I'M A MAN WHO HAPPENS TO BE BLACK

I'm a MAN *Who* Happens To Be BLACK

BRIAN BOLDEN

Bloomington, IN  Milton Keynes, UK

authorHOUSE®

AuthorHouse™
1663 Liberty Drive, Suite 200
Bloomington, IN 47403
www.authorhouse.com
Phone: 1-800-839-8640

AuthorHouse™ *UK Ltd.*
500 Avebury Boulevard
Central Milton Keynes, MK9 2BE
www.authorhouse.co.uk
Phone: 08001974150

This book is a work of non-fiction. Unless otherwise noted, the author and the publisher make no explicit guarantees as to the accuracy of the information contained in this book and in some cases, names of people and places have been altered to protect their privacy.

First published by AuthorHouse 7/13/2006

ISBN: 1-4259-4772-7 (sc)
ISBN: 1-4259-4773-5 (dj)

Library of Congress Control Number: 2006905824

Printed in the United States of America
Bloomington, Indiana

This book is printed on acid-free paper.

CONTENTS

AUTHOR'S NOTE	vii
SYNOPSIS	ix
INTRODUCTION	xiii
CHAPTER ONE	1
Holding Ourselves Accountable?	2
You Never Know Who's Watching	4
Don't Tear Me Down	7
A Foreign Reality	11
Life On The Other Side	16
CHAPTER TWO	19
Living In The Past	19
Be A Role Model	22
I've Been Stripped	24
Spirituality Loves Forgiveness	28
Success Is A Possibility	32
Let It Go	36
A Strange Mindset	38
Do The Right Thing	39
Reality Check	41

Chapter Three   43

  Selective Prejudice   43

  A Different Kind of Color Blind   45

  Lending a Helping Hand   48

  Experiencing Different Cultures   52

  No Color?   53

  The Wrong Expectations   56

Chapter Four   59

  Change Brings about Change   60

Chapter Five   67

  What Are We Teaching Our Children?   67

  The Wrong Kind of Support   74

Chapter Six   81

  Find The Positive In a Negative Situation   81

  What Will Our Children Choose?   86

  Choosing Success   88

Chapter Seven   91

  A Woman's Perspective   91

Epilogue   101

Acknowledgments   109

AUTHOR'S NOTE

As a man who happens to be black, I've learned over the years the significance of communication. I believe as a human race, we can keep hope alive if we all just get along.

Somebody once said, if you are going to copy someone, just make sure you copy the right person for the right reason. So I emulate Rodney King when he states, "Can't we all just get along?" when I made the decision years ago to simply my life by trying to get along with everyone. The reality is, men were created equal. If we as a human race would forgive others one third as much as Jesus forgives us, there would be very little prejudice, racism, jealousy, and envy.

I emulate Reverend Jesse Jackson when he states "Keep hope alive" when I put my pride aside and understood that it was okay to ask for help, and by asking for help it didn't make me any less of a man, but made me the man I needed to become.

In order to be a man, I realized I must first love myself, be myself in order to please myself. As a result, I demand the respect of others around me to accept me as I am. But most importantly, it gives me the power, authority, and confidence in myself not to allow others to influence, determine, or shape my behavior and individuality.

After graduating from Lamar University with a degree in communication, I realized my call and purpose in life is helping others. Just like Dr. Martin Luther King, I also have a dream that more men who view themselves as men who happen to be black, reach out and help men who view themselves as black men and niggas change their mentality, thought process, and mindset so they too may one day become successful men who happen to be black.

I have a dream that one day, we all come to the conclusion that no particular race is better than any other, because we are all part of the human race.

Lastly, I have a dream that we as a human race become color blind, because even if many of us didn't like each other, at least we would know that is wasn't because of the color of our skin.

The reality is, men were created equal, but it's unfortunate that we don't use what we were created with.

SYNOPSIS

I have been asked many times, what inspired me to write this book. As a man who happens to be black, I saw a race of people falling by the wayside and still living in bondage because of their mentality, thought process, and mindset. I know I can't save the world, the whole African-American race or the whole human race. However, I know I must make every effort to make a difference by helping as many as I can. I can no longer sit back and watch so many African-American men continue to be filled with jealousy, envy, prejudice, hate, and racism because they let the past dictate their view of themselves as black men. So many African Americans continue to hinder themselves from becoming successful because of their mentality, thought process, and mindset. As a race, we must come to the realization that slavery is over and we can no longer hold the entire Caucasian race of today responsible for what their parents and grandparents did to our parents and grandparents. It is imperative that we realize and understand that we can control our own destiny by changing our mentality, thought process, and mindset. In my efforts to help millions of people, I wrote this book to appeal to the masses of people from all races, cultures and environments by:

1. Helping those who view themselves as black men understand that once they view themselves as men first, who happen to be black, they are no longer in bondage. The doors of opportunities open because they don't see color, just another man who happens to be black, white, brown, or whatever color they may be.

2. Helping women of all races realize and understand what type of men they are dating or getting involved with, a black man, nigga, or a man who happens to be black. After reading this book, women will be able to make better choices and judgments when selecting a mate, because they will know exactly who they are dealing with up front, based on the characteristics, behaviors, mentalities, thought processes, and mindsets that I have explained in this book.

3. Helping men of all races understand that we are responsible for nurturing, molding, monitoring, instilling, and shaping our children's mentality, thought process, and mindset, not society.

4. Helping all races to understand that what we instill in our children now will determine who they become as adults. If we are not responsible parents, our children will become another statistic.

5. Helping all races understand that it doesn't matter where you were born; you can overcome any condition, situation, or circumstance.

6. Helping other races to understand why many African Americans think the way they think, act the way they act, and do the things they do.

7. Helping all races realize and understand that culture, environment, success, spirituality, love, and forgiveness have no color, nor do they belong to any specific race. They belong to all races, because the reality is, we are all part of the **human race.**

8. Helping many African Americans understand that we can no longer hold the entire Caucasian race responsible for what their parents and grandparents did because they had nothing to do with it.

9. Helping to break down racial barriers by not seeing color, but seeing an individual as simply a man or woman.

10. Helping to demonstrate that it is time we all come together and do our part by being helpers one to another.

As a human race, we must become color blind and see each other as simply men and women who happen to be black, white, brown, or whatever color they may happen to be. I am sure of this one thing: Jesus is coming back, and if you make it to heaven on Judgment Day,

I can promise you there will be no more jealousy, envy, hate, prejudice, or racism. There will be nothing but **love**. So as a human race, starting today, let's all make an asserted effort to make Jesus proud by taking advantage of the opportunity that he gave us, **life.**

INTRODUCTION

JESUS FED A MULTITUDE OF people (5,000) with five loaves of bread and two fish. He also created us in his own image. In my own efforts to emulate Jesus, I wrote this book to also feed a multitude of people, but to also appeal to the masses of people from different races, cultures, and environments. Before you read this book, I ask that you please pray first and ask that God would open your mind, heart, and soul so that you may receive what God has placed in my heart and spirit to write.

As members of the human race, we must realize and understand that we all have room for change and improvement, and many of us need to change and improve as individuals in many areas of our lives. After reading this book, I have no doubt in my mind that it will change millions of people's mentality, thought process, and mindset.

Because of the struggles that our parents and grandparents had to endure, I am very grateful, thankful, and appreciative. My research increased my gratitude and respect for the battles they fought. We now have choices and opportunities that we would not have had, if it had not been for them.

As a race, we must be dedicated and committed to making sure that we make better choices and take advantage of every opportunity that was made possible by our parents and grandparents.

I hope and pray this book will help free millions of people who are still full of envy, jealousy, hate, prejudice, and racism get past deep-rooted issues that have held them in mental bondage all their lives.

Whether you view yourself as a "black man" or a "man who happens to be black," we must all be open to change and improving ourselves as men, because it is never too late to become a better person or successful, since love, success, and forgiveness have no color or time limit.

I pray that after reading this book, you become a new person with a new mentality, thought process, and mindset; a person with a new destiny and finally a newfound success that was made, in part, by the struggles of our parents and grandparents.

I'M A MAN
WHO HAPPENS TO BE
BLACK

CHAPTER ONE

WHEN GOD CREATED THE HEAVENS and the earth, he also created male and female. Before I was born, God predestined me to be a male. After I was born, it was determined and confirmed, first by God and then the doctor, that I was a male. I was an infant who became a toddler, an adolescent, a teenager, and then a man. There is a reality that will never change: I am black. Long before becoming a man, I went through this thing called life that made me the man I am today. As a man who happens to be black, I often wondered, "What is a black man?" After looking up the word "black" in the dictionary, I knew from that point on and that day forward, I didn't want to be viewed, nor do I view myself, as a black man. For those of you who don't know, *black is defined as "opposite of white, dark-complexioned, Negro, dirty, evil, wicked, disgraceful, angered, and without hope."* First of all, I am a human being, and secondly, I am a man who just happens to be black. Black is the opposite of white, and I am dark-complexioned, however I am not a Negro, nor am I in any way dirty, evil, wicked, disgraceful, angered, or without hope. I refuse to view, associate, disgrace, or belittle myself with anything negative in any way, shape, form, or fashion.

HOLDING OURSELVES ACCOUNTABLE?

After numerous interviews and months of research, I realized that there is a different mentality, thought process, and mindset between a man who views himself as a black man and a man who views himself as a man who happens to be black. I found that men who view themselves as a black man take pride in being black, while men who view themselves as a man who happens to be black take pride in just simply being a man first.

As a race, it is very important and imperative that we take pride in ourselves, our heritage and culture, because we are who we are due to the struggles that our parents and foreparents went through to shed the derogatory terms (nigger and nigga) used to describe those of us with the darker complexion. Over time, we have become desensitized to the pain that those terms have caused. Growing up as a child, we were all taught certain morals and values, whether good or bad. As African Americans, we experienced growing up in different environments, backgrounds, and for many, even different cultures.

Nevertheless, as children, we were only taught what our parents and foreparents knew, which at that time may not have been much; however, they did the best they could. Unfortunately, racism and prejudice were also taught and instilled in many African Americans because of the past.

After becoming adults, many of us now realize that some of the things that we were taught by our parents and foreparents were incorrect, **through no fault of their own.** It is important that we understand we cannot blame our parents for what we were taught, because they were only able to teach us what their parents taught them. Many of us now have the education, power, authority, opportunity, and knowledge to make a difference by changing our mentality, thought process, and mindset. However, as adults, we continue to do things that we were taught as children, that we now know are wrong, instead of trying to correct the problem by holding ourselves responsible and accountable for what we know is wrong.

At what point in our lives do we grow up and take responsibility for continuing to do what we know is wrong? The answer is this: When we finally view ourselves as simply men who happen to be black, we will become accountable for our actions. Many who view themselves as black men have the mentality that they should only live in the black culture and environment, instead of living in the world that consists of men who happen to be black, white, Hispanic, and so on. Because of our parents and foreparents, we now have an opportunity to simply become men **without any restrictions.**

As long as African-American men continue to view themselves as black men, many will continue to have a "slave," "crab-in-the-bucket" and "the white man is always trying to keep a black man down" mentality. However, the reality is, the black man is keeping the black man down because of his black-man mentality. As a race, we must set standards for ourselves as an individual, but most importantly, see ourselves as more than just a black man or nigga. It's time many of us realize that being professional, polite, diverse, considerate and classy is not just for women. All too often, many African-American men feel like they have to portray a hardcore persona in order to feel like a man. The reality is, a real man doesn't have any problem with another man knowing that he is polite, considerate, or sensitive, because he realizes that he is human and he has feelings, just like anyone else. As a race, we must come to the realization that we are not in prison, locked behind bars, so being "hard" doesn't make you a man, and just because a real man doesn't portray a "hardcore" persona, it doesn't make him soft or any less of a man. As men, we must stop stereotyping specific characteristics and behaviors, because it hinders your ability to relate to your full capacity, because you never know who's watching you. We must also realize that class and professionalism are not limited to one race, but open to all races.

YOU NEVER KNOW WHO'S WATCHING

While I was growing up, my mother would tell me and my brothers to always carry ourselves in a classy and professional manner, because you never know who's watching you. In 1991, that statement became a reality. During Christmas break my senior year in college, I went to Austin, Texas to visit my brother, who was a probation officer at a juvenile detention facility. After showing me around the facility, he took me to meet Mr. Barker, who was the facility director at the time. While conversing, we talked about several things, and eventually got around to talking about me in general. I mentioned that I played basketball at Lamar University, and during my spare time, I would go to the high schools and junior high schools, talking to students and student athletes about drug awareness and alcohol. I also mentioned that I would have basketball camps for underprivileged children during the summers. He then made the statement, "You seem to be good with kids," and I replied by saying, "I love giving back to the community by helping others." He then told me if I wanted a job after I graduated, he would definitely hire me.

After graduating, I immediately moved to Austin, Texas, and Mr. Barker hired me as a juvenile probation officer, just as he said he would. After being there for only eight months, a supervisor's position became available, and Mr. Barker told me to apply for the position. I applied for the position and went through the interview process, but I didn't get the position, which was okay with me. I realized that I had only been there for eight months, so I was just happy that Mr. Barker had asked me to apply, not to mention to also get an interview. Approximately three months later, another supervisor's position became available, and again Mr. Barker told me to apply, which I did. Once again, I went through the interview process, but this time I got the position. One week later, Mr. Barker called me to his office. He told me the reason I didn't get the position the first time was because he wanted me to go through the interview process, so I would be prepared the next time a position became available. He then went on to tell me that he had been watching me for six months and he was impressed with my professionalism and the way I carried myself. I'm proud to inform you that Mr. Barker is man who happens to be Caucasian.

In 1992, that statement became another reality. I wanted to open another bank account, so I decided to join Travis County Credit Union. I really enjoyed being a member, because everyone was so nice and they gave me personal attention whenever I went to make a transaction. I eventually got to know everyone on a personal level, from the president to the tellers. Approximately four years later, I was in my car, sitting in a drive-through lane, filling out a deposit slip, when someone knocked on my window. It was Margaret Rhoades, who was the president of the credit union. After a brief greeting and conversation, she told me she wanted me to be a member of the board of directors for the credit union. She asked me to come inside and fill out an application, which I did. As we continued to talk, she told me that she had been watching me every since I had become a member. She also told me that I always carry myself in a professional manner and she thought that I would be an asset to the credit union by being a member of the board. After the yearly meeting was held, it was official: I became a board member for Travis County Credit Union. For those who care to know, Margaret Rhoades is a woman who happens to be Caucasian and is currently still the president at Travis County Credit Union. **Once again, you never know who's watching you.**

As a race, it is time we stop making excuses by blaming others, and get out of "the white man is always trying to keep a black man down" mentality. The reality is, many African Americans are their own worst enemy; we believe that we won't get hired because of the color of our skin, but the person conducting the interviews is only concerned about you being qualified for the position. As a race, we must become more positive and realize there are a lot of men and women who happen to be Caucasian, who will hire men who happen to be black, because they are qualified and they carry themselves in a professional and classy manner; it has nothing to do with the color of their skin. **I'm a man who happens to be black, and I made up my mind years ago that I wouldn't allow the color of my skin to determine my individuality, success, or destiny.** Oftentimes, many African-American men will not even apply for certain positions because they mentally talk themselves out of the job. They are so concerned about not getting hired because of the color of their skin, instead of being confident and seeing themselves as qualified for the position.

Don't Tear Me Down

As a race, many African-American men continue to struggle with their identity because of our past, lack of knowledge, lack of education, and refusal to expose themselves to anything else outside of the black culture and black environment. The word *"past" is defined as "gone by, ended, or a former time."* Although no one can physically live in the past, so many African-American men continue to mentally live and hold on to the past, which makes it impossible to move forward in life.

Instead of continuing to mentally live in the past, as a race we must be thankful, appreciative, and grateful for the struggles of our parents and foreparents, because we now have opportunities available to us that we otherwise would not have had, if it had not been for them.

I wholeheartedly believe that it is an insult to our parents and grandparents when we, as a race, do not utilize and take advantage of the opportunities that they made possible for us. As a race, we must take advantage of the right to view ourselves as simply a man who happens to be black, instead of continuing to struggle with our identity of still seeing ourselves as a black man or nigga. If we continue to hold on to our past and mentally live in a former time that has gone by and ended, then the cycle will never be broken, and so many African-American men will continue to live in bondage. Many who view themselves as a black man often see color, and therefore may become prejudiced, because you see a man who happens to be black as a black man or nigga, a man who happens to be white as a white man or honky, and a man who happens to be Hispanic as a Mexican or spic, instead of simply seeing that individual as a man.

Many men who view themselves as black men focus on wanting people to know that they are black men. The majority of men who view themselves as a black man continue to struggle with their identity, normally stemming from our past or having a bad experience with someone of a different race, which usually seems to be with a Caucasian. They also have a tendency to tear down, belittle, and talk negatively about other African-American men who are successful or striving to become successful. I also noticed they showed signs of jealousy and envy toward men who possess nice things, such as extravagant homes and expensive automobiles.

I remember talking to Dwayne, who was an associate of mine who is definitely pro-black and views himself as a black man. One day, I decided to call Dwayne to see how he was doing. He told me he was getting ready to leave because a friend called and wanted him to go to the mall to analyze and talk about other African Americans.

I immediately asked him "Why would you do something like that? It's nothing positive about it." I told him that a lot of people do not have much at all, and that's all they may have to wear, but they are doing the best they can. I told him that just because God has blessed him to be able to wear nice clothes, it doesn't make him better than anyone else. I also told him to remember that he may be in that same situation one day. I then asked him why he and his friend were being so negative toward people who have never said or done anything to them. I then told him instead of being negative, why don't he and his friend go to the mall and do something productive and meaningful by being positive and encouraging people by talking with them instead of talking about them. After talking to Dwayne, he said, "You're right, I shouldn't do that, because it's not nice.

For whatever reason, many African Americans find pleasure in belittling and tearing down other African Americans. I truly believe that many of them find satisfaction in tearing down others because of their jealousy, envy, and their own personal failures. For many, being negative and tearing down others is fun because just for that brief moment, they feel like they are better than someone else. The reality is, it's nothing more than a false sense of satisfaction, because no one is better than anyone else; God created us all equal. The problem is, many African Americans do not see themselves as men; instead, they see themselves as black men and niggas, so therefore it is impossible for them to see themselves as an equal. Unfortunately, many African Americans have low self-esteem, which contributes to many of us continuing to still mentally live in the past.

It is amazing how easily we embrace being negative, but treat being positive like it's the AIDS disease. Being negative doesn't require much energy, but being positive requires complimenting and encouraging others. But it's very hard to compliment and encourage someone else when you are jealous and envious of them. As a race, we must realize that being negative is a disease that is very infectious, and ultimately leads to a slow and painful death. We must also realize that life has far too much to offer. We should enjoy life to the fullest and begin to find satisfaction in being positive, and live a productive, meaningful life.

Many African-American men have lost sight of the foundation for life, **spirituality**. For many, being negative has become a good thing, and being positive has become a sin. **In short, many seem to make God sin and the devil good, as opposed to making God good and the devil sin. Many African-American men are quick to call Caucasians devils, but a lot of us are devils as well, because the reality is, the devil does not belong to one specific race, but exists in all races.**

After many hours of hanging out and conversing with hundreds of men who view themselves as black men, I found that many of them were extremely negative and took great pride in also referring to themselves as a "nigga." I noticed it was just a part of their daily vocabulary and conversation. As far as their behavior, many of them were very rude, extremely loud, disrespectful, unappreciative, and inconsiderate of others. I was shocked, but more disappointed to see that when they had encounters with other African-American men who were successful, sensitive, understanding, professional, well-spoken, respectful, and considerate, they saw them as being soft and stated "They must be gay."

I then questioned and challenged their statements, mindsets, and thought processes, because I am a successful, sensitive, understanding, professional, well-spoken, respectful, and considerate man, and I am not soft, nor am I gay.

It was very disappointing and disturbing to see the way many African-American men view other African-American men who do not have their same characteristics and exhibit their same behavior. For those of you men who view themselves as a black man or a nigga, please know and understand that just because a man views himself as a man who happens to be black, does not act the way you act, speak the way you speak, or do the things you do, it doesn't make him soft, gay, or any less of a man.

A FOREIGN REALITY

As I continued my research, I found that those who took great pride in viewing themselves as a nigga were the worst of the worst and the lowest of the low within the African-American race. I never thought I would see the day when any man would proudly and boldly call himself a nigga, thug, and hoodlum, and take pride in saying it. I noticed that they have absolutely no morals, values, consideration, concern, or respect for themselves, their parents, or anyone else. Their mentality is, it's all about survival, and only the strong will survive. I noticed an extremely high majority of them have quick tempers and have no problem with cursing out their parents or anyone else. They are extremely loud, rude, ignorant, and have very little or no patience. The majority of them are not even remotely interested in diversity or exposing themselves to other cultures and environments. I noticed that many of them have a one-track mind and refuse to compromise. Their mentality is, it's their way or no way at all.

I found an extremely high majority are irrational, very negative, and have a very bad understanding about everything in life in general. They also have no problem with fighting and possibly killing someone over something as simple as a domino, basketball, or card game. The majority of them are unemployed and still live at home with their parents as an adult. I was amazed to find that many of them never went outside of a thirty to fifty-mile radius from where they live. Although an extremely high majority only had a seventh-grade education, many of them willingly admitted they would rather not work at all, or sell drugs, rather than work an eight-to-five job paying minimum wage. Many of them stated working an eight-to-five job is chump change and they refuse to work for the white man. I found that many of them had been to prison and had no problem with going back if need be. I was absolutely astounded by how many of them stated they had no fear of dying and had no problem killing someone.

Approximately 98 percent stated they hate Caucasians and viewed all of them as devils. I noticed that the majority of them were very violent and had no problem with physically abusing women. Approximately 97 percent referred to women as "bitches" and stated they were only good for three things: sex, cooking, and having babies. They took great pride in constantly being negative, because they had nothing to look forward to or to live for. Many of them stated that they didn't live day by day, they lived minute by minute.

Approximately 98 percent stated that honesty and loyalty didn't exist in their world because it was every man for himself. I was amazed to find that many of them could not read or could barely read. I was also amazed to find that some of them didn't have a driver's license, identification card, or a social security number.

As a man who happens to be black, I was truly saddened to see the number of African-American men who had no hope or desire to see themselves as men or think success is even remotely possible. From a personal standpoint, I couldn't image or begin to understand how any human being could have that type of mentality and function on a day-to-day basis. **The unfortunate reality is, my world is just as foreign to them as theirs is to me.**

That is why it is so important that we as men who happen to be black adopt the **"each one teach one mentality,"** by taking one person who views himself as a nigga under your wing and try to help him change his mentality, thought process, and mindset. The harsh reality is, those who view themselves as a nigga oftentimes infect and affect the entire African American race. Oftentimes, people of a different race think African Americans are all the same because of the behavior and attitude of those who view themselves as a nigga, when in actuality, it does not represent who many of us are at all. I used to wonder why women of different races would grab or hold on to their purse extremely tightly when an African-American male would walk by or get close to them. In all honesty, it used to offend me, but as I have matured and become wiser, it's sad to say, but I understand why. Unfortunately, men who view themselves as a nigga have made it hard for many of us who view ourselves as simply men who just happen to be black.

In all honesty, I must admit I sometimes feel uneasy if I'm around a group of men who view themselves as a nigga, especially if I don't know any of them and they don't know me, because I feel like anything could happen, so I fear the unknown. Because of their mentality and behavior in public, there have been many times when I have been ashamed, embarrassed, wanted to crawl under a table, and even wished I could turn into a bird so I could fly away immediately, simply because they have absolutely no respect for themselves or others around them.

During my research, I found that men who view themselves as a nigga felt like all African Americans are supposed to view themselves in that same manner. When I questioned their mentality, they all stated, "This is a white man's world and you are just another nigga just like me in the eyes of the white man." After hearing several others' statements, I explained to them the positive experiences I've had with men and women who happen to be Caucasian. Many of them stated, "A white man has never helped me," and I reply by saying, "The reason a man who happens to be Caucasian has never helped you is because you have never given one an opportunity to help you, because you have never exposed yourself to anything else outside of the African-American culture." Surprisingly, many of them said I was right, but they also stated that they would have to see it to believe it. I tried to leave them with hope by telling them all Caucasians are not devils, and they should not allow their condition and circumstance to stop them from becoming successful. I also told them if they change their mentality, thought process, and mindset, they could control their own destiny.

While having conversations with associates I have personally known for years, I have been told on several occasions that I talk and act white. On occasion, they tease me about my mannerisms, the fact that I speak proper English, and have done well for myself. I noticed they would always say it in a joking manner, but I knew they were serious, and deep down inside, they really meant every word.

Nevertheless, I would always reply by asking, "How does a white person act and talk?" and to no surprise, they could or would never answer the question. Nevertheless, I didn't take it to heart, nor did I take offense at it, because I had to consider the source from which the statement came.

Needless to say, such comments always came from someone who had limited education, was pro-black, and used slang and profanity constantly. It was also the ones who refer to themselves as a "nigga" and are content with making $9 per hour, staying at home with their parents as an adult or jobless.

However, I would always continue to encourage them, by letting them know that they can do whatever they choose to do and become whatever they choose to become, if they mentally dedicated and committed themselves to becoming successful. The sad and unfortunate thing is, it lets me know there are still a lot African-American men who still live in the past by thinking that all African Americans should have a poverty mentality.

I am amazed but truly saddened by the number of African-American men in this day and age who associate being successful and educated, and speaking proper English, with someone who is Caucasian.

Just to clarify, there is nothing Caucasian about me. I am simply a man who is educated and speaks proper English. I am a man who is completely happy with himself, his individuality, personality, and spirituality, and I just happen to be black. As a race, many of us must get out of this poverty mentality and get to a point in our lives where we realize, understand, and believe that speaking proper English, getting an education, and becoming successful is not just limited to one race, but open to all races.

For whatever reason, many African-American men who refer to themselves as a black man or nigga normally try to portray a "Mr. Tough Guy" persona to show people how tough they think they are, because they associate being a man with being tough.

As a race, we must understand that the best way to prove you are a man is to just simply be a man. A real man doesn't feel like he has to prove he's a man, because he already knows he's a man.

Life On The Other Side

In my research, I found that men who view themselves as a man who happens to be black were mainly focused on their careers, being successful, and having a family. They were open to change and experiencing what life has to offer in general. The majority were extremely positive, successful, educated, respectful, well-spoken, considerate, appreciative, and professional. They were high on integrity and honesty.

I noticed that they were well-groomed, took pride in their appearance, and demanded their respect. They were very open-minded, diverse, and looked at themselves as being equal to all races because they put their pants on one leg at a time just like everyone else. They also took pride in carrying themselves in a professional manner.

I was thrilled to see how many of them used others' successes to encourage and motivate themselves to do better and become even more successful.

After many hours of hanging out and conversing with hundreds of men who view themselves as a man who happens to be black, I found an extremely high majority of them did not see color, because many of their counterparts were of a different race. They were also opened to being exposed to different cultures and environments, because they stated success has no color, limits, or boundaries.

Many of them stated that if they had not been open to being exposed to different cultures and environments, they would not be where they are today. The majority stated that there is nothing specific that represents any particular culture or race when you simply see yourself as just a man. So therefore, when they felt like doing something, they just did it without labeling or associating it with any particular race or culture.

The majority of them also stated that they prefer being exposed to different cultures and environments, because culture is not limited to one race, but open to all races. I found that many of them take advantage and utilize being exposed to different cultures and environments to open doors. Several of them made profound statements by saying that many African Americans have the key to closed doors that are already open for them, but because of their mentality, thought process, and mindset, they keep the doors locked themselves.

As African-American men, many of us have so much potential and don't even realize it. But because of our mentality, thought process, and mindset many of us do not reach our full potential. We must come to the understanding that change equals opportunities, and opportunities equal success. In 1997, I worked at a car dealership with a man Dwayne who was pro-black and definitely viewed himself as a black man.

He was extremely gifted and talented and his potential was unlimited. Dwayne had the look, personality, charisma, and intelligence, but he was lacking in the area that mattered the most: his attitude. Although Dwayne had many attributes, he was one of the most negative individuals I had encountered in quite some time. If he wasn't tearing down other African-American men, he would be talking negative about Caucasians. I didn't like talking to Dwayne much, because whatever it was that he was going to be talking about,

I knew it was going to be negative. It didn't matter where he was or who was around him, he would always use profanity and refer to African Americans as niggas. For several years, I tried to help Dwayne with his attitude, because I saw he had the potential to become very successful in this business. I constantly stressed to him that his attitude, mentality, thought process, and mindset controls his destiny. I would always tell him that he would not reach his full potential until he changed his attitude and mentality. I told him if he would exert that same energy into being as positive as he currently is negative, he would double his production. I told him he had too much potential to just be selling eight cars a month. I told him to just try changing his attitude for a month and see if it makes a difference in his sales, because he had nothing to lose but all to gain. I explained to him that when you are constantly being negative, it carries over into everything you do in life. I told him that negativity is a disease that carries a deadly infection. Dwayne had been negative for so many years, he didn't even realize he was being negative. After constantly talking to Dwayne, he told me that he was going to make an effort to change his attitude and mentality, because he had nothing to lose. The following month, he sold sixteen cars, and from that point on, he sold fifteen consistently. Eight months later, Dwayne was making a six-figure income as sales manager.

The moral to this story is, when Dwayne decided to change his attitude and mentality, it changed his life. Dwayne is no longer a black man, but a man who happens to be black, and one who has become successful.

CHAPTER TWO

LIVING IN THE PAST

As I CONTINUED TO RESEARCH the differences between the two, I found that many men who see themselves as being a black man normally associate the word *black* with our past. When you look at our past, it represents slavery, bondage, and oppression. Men who view themselves as a black man normally do not see themselves as being a man first, because they are so focused on proving to the world that they are black. They were not open to doing anything outside of their black culture or environment.

In addition, an extremely high majority of them were not successful, and did not ever see themselves becoming successful, because they felt someone else was holding them back (the white man), when in actuality, they were holding themselves back because of their mentality, thought process, and mindset.

As humans, many of us do not realize the power of mentality, thought process and mindset.

What do I mean by mentality, thought process, and mindset? Let's think about each term separately and then apply them to the problems of prejudice and racism.

Mentality refers to a person's mental capacity. How much is he willing and able to learn? Is he willing to take risks and try new experiences, or is he happy to maintain his present level of knowledge or ignorance? For example, a man might complain that he can't get a decent job because he is black, but the reality may be that he lacks the skill to do the job he would like to have.

Depending on his mentality, he will either stay put and continue to complain, or he will go to college or take other training that will give him the skills he need. But the first step may be to expand his mentality.

Thought process refers to the way a person's brain operates, perceives, or views. How does he perceive himself and the world around him? How does he relate information and experiences to himself? When something goes wrong in his life, does he interpret the situation as a personal insult or as just something that happen to anybody? Does he solve problems by thinking them through, or does he expect other people to solve his problems?

Mindset refers to a person's mental attitude that determines a certain response. For example, if a person has decided that he doesn't like pancakes, the best pancakes in the world won't taste good to him. But if he has the mindset that he is open to experiences, he will try pancakes and then decide whether he likes them. Somebody once said that "attitude determines altitude," and that's probably true. People can usually accomplish what they have set their minds to accomplish.

As humans, we all know that we have the ability to control our mentality, thought processes and mindsets. However, many African Americans have what I call "selective thought process and mindset," which means we utilize and control our thought process and mindset when we choose to do so. It's amazing how we can move on from bad relationships, divorces, and the death of a loved one, but we can't move on from our past that many of us never even experienced.

As African Americans, our parents and foreparents had their mentality determined by social conditions based on slavery, prejudice, and limitations on their ability to change their condition. So therefore, I can understand our parents and foreparents still having that mentality, simply because they lived it every day.

James Mitchell, who is my uncle, states, "I worked in the fields twelve hours a day, picking and baling cotton for fifty cents a day." He told me that on Saturdays he worked in the boss's house, and on Sundays at noon, the boss would take all his workers to town for a couple of hours.

He told me that he had one pair of pants to wear on Sundays and three pair of pants to wear during the week. He also told me that he didn't get a chance to go to school until he was fourteen years old, because he had to work in the cotton fields. He also told me that his boss had given him a female hog and told him he could make extra money by breeding the hog and selling the babies. Eventually, his hog had babies, and when he came to work one day, his boss had sold the hog and the babies and never gave him a dime. He told me that his boss had given him two acres of land, which he plowed and cropped. After he plowed and cropped the land, he came to work one day, only to find that his boss had sold his land. He states, although that was a bad time in his life, things have changed for the better. He also states, "I have no bitterness or anger toward the entire Caucasian race, because I have met many Caucasians who are good people and have helped me in many ways."

The reality is, many African Americans will never change their mentality because of all they had to endure. However, there are many who are able to adapt and make the change. My point is this: If my uncle, who actually lived it every day, can move on from his past, why is it so difficult for our generation to move on from a past that they never experienced?

The torch has now been passed on to our generation, and we must break the cycle and make a difference. However, it is hard to break a cycle in a race of people who don't physically live in the past, but still continue to mentally live in the past.

The sad thing is, many African-American men are not even remotely interested in trying to change or become a better person, because for many, change takes far too much work and energy, so it's easier to just stay the way they are. As a race, many African-American men are happy and content in some aspects of their lives, but miserable and dissatisfied in others.

Be A Role Model

Many African-American men want to change, but as individuals, we are not willing to do what it takes to make the change happen. The problem is, we want change to happen without having to work or do anything for it. In short, we want something for nothing. We must realize and understand that change brings about change. However, there are many who were able to adapt and make the change from being a black man or nigga to becoming a man who happens to be black. Once we reach that point in our lives, it is very important that we never forget where we came from. Oftentimes, many African Americans change for the worst after experiencing years of success. It is imperative that we remember that there was a time when many of us viewed ourselves as black men and niggas. We must now reach out and help them change their mentality, thought process, and mindset and begin to see themselves as men who happen to be black. It is time for men who happen to be black to give back to the African-American race, so that others may also have the same opportunities that we now have, because the reality is, many of us didn't get where we are today by ourselves, there were people who helped us along the way.

Whether we like it or not, as men who happen to be black, the torch has been passed on to us, and we must now become role models. Therefore, we are responsible for keeping hope alive within the African-American race.

As a race, we must be more empathetic, compassionate, patient, and understanding, because there are a lot of African-American men who really and truly want to change and become men who happen to be black. The problem is, many of them have no earthly idea where to begin, while others have far too much pride because in their mind, it shows a sign of weakness, which equates to being less of man. We must open the lines of communication and give them a starting point.

As men, we must begin to understand that it's okay to ask for help, and just because you ask for help, it doesn't make you any less of a man. In actuality, once you get to the point in your live where you put your pride aside and don't mind asking for help, it's only then that you become a man.

Once you become a man and begin to view yourself as a man who happens to be black, just make sure that you don't forget where you came from. Then you must reciprocate the favor and do the same thing for someone else, just as someone did the same for you.

As a race, if we continue to do the same things today that we were doing ten years ago, and have the same mentality that our parents and foreparents have, how can we expect our present situation to ever change. As a race, we must realize that it is not possible to live a productive and meaningful life or become successful in today's society, if we are still living in bondage by mentally living in the past.

I've Been Stripped

It is a fact that the thought processes and mindsets that our parents and foreparents instilled in many of us contribute to the cycle that has been passed on from generation to generation and has never been broken and still exists today. **The reality is, many of our parents and foreparents were stripped of their dignity and manhood, which ultimately led many of them to have low self-esteem and no self-worth.**

Without their dignity and manhood, they had very little to instill in our parents, but they gave what little they had left to give.

Unfortunately, many African-American men of our generation have no morals, values, character, dignity, spirit, or self-respect. Society tells African-American men that their only self-worth is in the bedroom; because of this mentality, there are many African-American men who can't look others (especially Caucasians) eye to eye without putting their heads down.

After conversing with hundreds of men who view themselves as a black man, many of them stated they felt uncomfortable being around Caucasians, and only dealt with them if it was absolutely necessary. I was astounded when many of them willingly admitted that they were intimidated by Caucasians, mainly in the work environment, because they saw them as being powerful.

I realized the truth of this perception, although many African Americans will not willingly admit it. I have seen many African Americans who get nervous at work when someone Caucasian comes around.

These are normally the same African Americans who want and ask for the same advice ten times from family members and friends, but will never use the advice given to them. However, when they ask that same question to someone Caucasian who gives them the same advice one time, they do it, simply because they view Caucasians as being more powerful.

Many of them even made the statement "This is a white's man world." First of all, this is God's world and he rules the heavens and the earth and everything in between. Secondly, this is not a white man's world, because God's world consists of people who happen to be black, white,

brown, and so on. This world belongs to no particular race, but consists of all races.

As a race, it is time that we realize and understand that the price has been paid, and paid in full indeed, by our parents and foreparents. We must now pick up our heads, have dignity, show spirit, and show that we have self-worth that extends past the bedroom.

The change will not be easy because as a race, many African Americans have been infected, effected, and affected.

Infected is defined as contaminated with disease or to cause to become diseased.

Many African-American men have been infected because they have adopted our parents' and foreparents' mentality. Our parents and foreparents have instilled their mentality in many of us, so now many of us have simply taken up where our parents and foreparents left off. Therefore, our minds are contaminated with hate, racism, and prejudice, which ultimately keeps you in bondage mentally, and hinders you from ever reaching your full potential, because you are not open to being exposed to anything other than the African-American culture and environment.

Effected is defined as anything brought about by cause or result and the power to bring about results.

Many African American men have been **effected** by the struggles of our parents and foreparent. When family members or a close friend get hurt, it is human nature and only natural that we also feel the hurt and pain that they are going through. But we also try to punish whoever hurt the person we care about. So as a result, many of us are now trying to make up for the hurt, pain, and struggles that our parents and foreparents suffered through our actions, by holding the entire Caucasian race responsible for the past. In doing so, it **effects** our mentality, thought process, and mindset, because the reality is, it keeps us in bondage mentally.

Affected is defined as strive after or to influence.

Now we must **affect** our children in a positive way. We must influence them to take advantage of the choices and opportunities that our parents and foreparents made possible by their hurt, pain, and struggles.

We must also influence them by teaching them morals, values, respect, responsibility, character, and most importantly, the fact that they are men who just simply happen to be black.

As a race, we can no longer afford to **infect** our children's mindsets. Instead we must **affect** their thought processes in a positive manner to ensure stronger mental **effects** so they will have a brighter future.

As a race, it is imperative and important that we realize and understand that we have a history to remember, but most importantly, a future to mold.

SPIRITUALITY LOVES FORGIVENESS

The time is now, that we as a race come to the conclusion that **spirituality, love, and forgiveness have no color, nor define any particular race, environment, or culture**. However, these are three major areas that we must be dedicated and committed to working on as a race. **Once we deal with these issues, it will change our mentality, thought process, and mindset, and in the end, we become individuals who then view ourselves as simply a man who happens to be black.**

For whatever reason, many African-American men have lost their zeal for spirituality. Although our parents and foreparents didn't have much to look forward to, **the majority of them definitely looked forward to attending church service, because that was one place they found peace and serenity**. For many African Americans, spirituality was one thing that our parents and foreparents knew to instill in many of us.

When I was growing up, my mother **made** my brothers and me go to church; it wasn't optional, it was **mandatory.** When I turned fourteen years old, my mother told me that she was not going to make me attend church anymore, because she had raised me to know right from wrong, and I knew I needed God in my life. After missing two straight Sundays, I felt guilty and found myself back in church. Even after I went off to college, I would still attend church on the Sundays that I didn't have basketball practice. After thirty-nine years, I still find myself attending church every Sunday. As a child, I really didn't realize and understand the importance of attending church and establishing a relationship with God for myself. However, as I got older, it became clear, and I thank God my mother **made** me attend church, because I know for a fact it made me the man I am today. **I am proud to say that I was called to the ministry approximately three years ago, and I am now a minister.**

Somewhere along the way, we as a race have lost sight of the foundation for life, **spirituality. As men who happen to be black, we must now be responsible men and become head of our households by going back to the times when having a bond and relationship with God was a priority.**

During my research, I found that the majority of men who view themselves as a black man do not attend or have not attended church service in many years. I also found there was a wide variety in their beliefs regarding spirituality because many of them know there is a God, while some don't believe in God and others stated that there is no God.

In life, there are things that are primary and secondary. I was amazed at the mentality that many of them had, because spirituality didn't even seem to be secondary.

On the other hand, I was not surprised to learn that men who view themselves as men who happen to be black stated that although they know that they do not live a perfect life, they still considered themselves Christians and normally attended church service on a regular basis. Many of them stated they wouldn't be where they are today if they didn't have God in their lives. Many of them also stated that their mentality, thought process, and mindset changed because of their **spirituality.** They also mentioned that it helped them to view others as simply an individual who is just a man, because spirituality and success has no color.

Secondly, the Bible says that we should **love** our neighbors as we **love** ourselves, and we are to help one another. For those who don't know, the Bible talks about **love** more than any other topic.

The problem with many African Americans is, we don't love ourselves, so therefore it is impossible to love our neighbors or anyone else. **As a race, we must realize, understand, and believe that love can overcome and conquer hate, prejudice, and racism.** The reality is, no one is perfect, but know that God still loves us in spite of all our sins and wrongdoings.

For many African Americans, **love** is selective and optional, which means we love whomever we choose to love when we choose to love them. As a race, we must adopt the mentality that love is mandatory, not optional. **However, we must get to a point in our lives where we love ourselves first, and only then can we begin to love others.**

We must understand that everything begins within and eventually works itself out through our actions. With this being the case, we might as well just love ourselves first, which ultimately leads to us being able to love others.

In my research, for whatever reason, I found that many men who view themselves as a black man or nigga actually do not love or respect themselves. For those of you who view yourself as a black man, you must simply see yourself as a man first, and with that comes a certain level of respect from others, and with respect comes love.

I found that men who view themselves as a man who happens to be black have no problem with loving and respecting themselves because they felt like they had no reason not to love and respect themselves or others.

Lastly, **forgiveness** is the beginning of a new life and the ending of an old life, simply because you are no longer holding yourself in bondage about our past. The Bible says Jesus will forgive us "seventy times seven." The Bible also tells us that Jesus created us in his own image, so we should at least try to be like him in some shape, form or fashion. **If we, as a race, would forgive others just a third as much as Jesus forgives us, there would be very little prejudice, racism, jealousy, and envy.**

I have often wished that God had made us all color blind when he created us, because even if many of us didn't like each other, at least we would know it wasn't because of the color of our skin.

As I continued my research, I noticed men who viewed themselves as black men found it very hard to forgive when it came to people of different races, especially the Caucasian race. I was under the impression that many of them felt like someone (mainly Caucasians) owed them something, and until they received what they felt was owed, they were not willing to forgive. However, I noticed that they found it easy to forgive when it came to other African Americans. Unfortunately, many African-American men continue to hold the entire Caucasian race responsible for our parents' and foreparents' past without realizing that the Caucasian race of today had nothing to do with what their parents and foreparents have done.

As a race, we must ask ourselves this question: "Where would we be if Jesus didn't forgive us?"

I noticed that the majority of men who view themselves as a man who happens to be black have somewhat mastered the art of forgiveness, because they realized if they didn't forgive by letting go of the past, they would still be in bondage mentally, which would hinder them from becoming successful.

Many of them stated that they didn't want to go through life with an unforgiving spirit, because then they would become focused on the past, which leads back to mentally being prejudiced and racist. Many of them stated they just want to get along with all races and continue to move forward with their lives, because success has no color. Many of them also mentioned that by not being forgiving, it would close the door to a lot of opportunities for success.

As a race, we must free our hearts, minds, and souls by learning to forgive others, just as Jesus forgives us.

However, after months of research, it is clearly evident why so many African Americans still view themselves as a black man or nigga, instead of viewing themselves as simply a man first, who happens to be black.

Success Is A Possibility

For many African-American men, success has become an impossible dream because the word *success* has never been a part of their vocabulary, thought process, or mindset. So therefore, they can only relate and be content with their current living environment, which isn't much, because that's all they know.

It is evident why many African-American men feel like they can't become successful, because they have an "I'm in a no-win situation" mentality. Many African-American men are content with where they are in life, because they see no way out, simply because they have never been taught anything else other than there is no way out.

The harsh reality is, many African American men do not have any type of positive role models in their lives, because no one in their family or no one close to them has ever been successful or striving to become successful, so therefore, they have no examples to follow, or no one to instill and encourage them to ever become successful.

So many African American men continue to fail in reaching their full potential and becoming successful, simply because they are so focused on the inevitabilities instead of the possibilities. The reality is, life has inevitabilities and we can't control it. Life also has possibilities, but we must first risk it.

The end result is, society then dictates and defines who they are as individuals. Black men can't succeed because they think of themselves as black men because society tells them they are black men. They then believe that success is not even an option or a possibility.

As African-American men, oftentimes we have a tendency to allow society's words to influence, determine, and shape our behavior and individuality. Many times we listen to other people tell us who we should be, what we should be, and how we should be instead of being who we are.

Then you become confused because you're trying to please everyone else by trying to be who they think you should be, and now you don't know who you are anymore. We must always realize that it doesn't matter what you do or how nice of a person you may be, it is not possible to please everybody.

If you are in this cycle, the first step toward success is this:

As a man, you must first love yourself, be yourself, in order to please yourself. As a result, you then demand the respect of others around you to accept you as you are. But most importantly, it gives you the power, authority, and confidence in yourself not to allow their words to influence, determine or shape your behavior and individuality.

As men, we must learn to always be ourselves, and if others like you, then great; if they don't like you, then that's great too. As men, we can no longer allow society's words to influence, determine, or shape who we are as a race, as an individual, or as a man who happens to be black.

As a race, we must understand that it is imperative that we shape and mold our children to view themselves as men first, but also instilling in them that they do have choices and opportunities to become whatever they choose to become.

As a race, we all have different perspectives and views regarding our past history and culture. As African Americans, many of us have now come to believe what so many others assume, simply because that's the only thing they know or have seen (television) regarding our culture, when in actuality, it may not represent who we really are at all.

However, as a race, many who view themselves as a black man or nigga have come to believe that all African Americans eat chicken and watermelon, and listen to rap music, because society tells us that. However, studies have shown, it is a fact that more Caucasian kids buy rap music than African Americans. Some things of culture are reality, however, culture should not be limited to just one race, but open to all races.

After talking to men who viewed themselves as black men, I found that they were so proud of being black that they formed cultural habits. Many of them had never seen anything outside of their culture, so therefore, cultural habits have become impossible to overcome or break.

I found that many who viewed themselves as black men were not sure of themselves and had low self-esteem as far as their feeling like they have the ability to be competitive in today's society.

I noticed that those who viewed themselves as being black men were very uncomfortable when having to participate in things outside the black culture or when dealing with others outside of their race.

When working on a job, I found that the majority of those who view themselves as black men feel like they are watched more closely because of the stigma of being a black man. I also found that while in the workplace, many of them felt intimidated, while men who viewed themselves as a man who happens to be black saw being watched as a challenge, and used that as a motivation factor.

As a race, we should expose ourselves and our children to all aspects of life and other cultures. People who view themselves as black focus on being black, acting black, and wanting people to know they're black, instead of focusing on exposing themselves to what life has to offer, in order to become more diverse in every aspect of their lives. Getting an education helps us to be more open-minded to being exposed to different things. As a race, we should all seek a Ph.D. in education and being exposed to different environments and cultures.

Let It Go

As I was writing this book, I decided to interview 200 men total, who view themselves as men who happen to be black and men who view themselves as just a black man. I asked the question: "If given the opportunity to experience living in our past for just one week, would you do it?" And they all said no.

I then asked the question: "Why do you continue to mentally live in the past?" What I found amazing was those who viewed themselves as a man who happens to be black stated that they do not live in the past, because the past is the past.

They also stated that since they did not live in that era, they really didn't know what it was like, but they could only imagine.

They mentioned that they only knew what they saw on television, and what they were told by their parents and grandparents.

It was concluded that they didn't want to focus or dwell on the past because they didn't want to have a one-track mind and mentality be held in bondage.

They also concluded that they would never forget our past but they didn't want to ever mentally live in our past because it would be a slap in the face and an insult to our parents and foreparents if we didn't take advantage of the opportunities that they made possible for our generation.

They all saw themselves as an equal, and refused to mentally live in the past because it would close the door for opportunities and hinder them from becoming successful. They felt if they constantly continued to mentally focus and dwell on the past, they would become their own worst enemy due to their mindset and thought process, which is the key to their destiny.

I found it equally amazing that men who viewed themselves as a black man constantly continued to focus and dwell on the past. After talking to those who consider themselves a black man, I was astounded by their mindset and thought process. I was in shock and disbelief when many of them stated, "I am still waiting on my forty acres and my mule that the white man promised me." First of all, even if that were true, it wasn't promised to anyone in our generation; it would have been promised to our foreparents and possibly our parents.

Secondly, why would you want a mule that you have absolutely no use for in this day and time, when you have a car to drive? I could only image the shame and disgrace of seeing African Americans riding around in Houston, Texas on mules.

Nevertheless, it lets me know that many African Americans still continue to hold on and live in the past.

For whatever reason, many African Americans still feel like the Caucasian race owes them something. Even if our parents and foreparents were promised forty acres and a mule, as a race, it is imperative that we realize and understand that the Caucasian race of today does not owe our generation anything; today's white men had nothing to do with what their parents and foreparents promised our parents and foreparents.

Yet many African Americans are still angry and hold the entire Caucasian race responsible for so-called unfulfilled promises that wasn't even promised to them; nor do they have a right or reason to be angry about it anyway.

A Strange Mindset

I was amazed at the number of men who refer to themselves as black men who viewed white men as devils. The thing that I found most amazing was that a majority of them had never even experienced a negative or bad encounter with a man who happened to be white. Because of their attitude, I was almost convinced that many of them had lived during that time or had encountered a really bad experience with someone of the Caucasian race, and to my surprise, they actually didn't.

However, those who did held the whole entire Caucasian race responsible for what one or two people have done.

I then asked those who view themselves as being a black man if they had ever had a negative encounter or bad experience with a man who happens to be black, and of course the answer was yes. Many even stated they had too many negative encounters and experiences to count. However, they still communicate, associate, and embrace the whole entire African-American race. Little do we know, it shows just how prejudiced many of us can be, as we are willing to accept the negative encounters from our own race and move on as though nothing ever happened. It is because they viewed their own as a man who happened to be black, or was it because he was a black man? Whatever the case may be, we do know this: they didn't hold the whole African-American race responsible for what one or two black men have done.

So, why are we so forgiving toward our own but not forgiving toward others? I applaud our race for being so forgiving and not holding the entire race responsible for what one or two men who happen to be black have done. So, why is it so hard for men who consider themselves black men to be forgiving and adopt that same mentality when it comes to men who happen to be white. I wholeheartedly believe the solution is this: We need to simply just view each other as men first, who just happen to be black, white, brown, or whatever color they happen to be.

When you view a person as a man, the best part is, you see no color, just an individual, just a man. In addition, when you see another individual as just a man first, then everyone becomes an equal.

Do The Right Thing

I remember my junior year in high school, a friend and I were walking through the parking lot when we noticed a small group of approximately eight African Americans in a circle. We knew it had to be someone fighting, but we didn't know who it was. When we reached the group of people, we noticed it was an African-American kid fighting a Caucasian kid. After a couple of seconds, everybody jumped in and started hitting and kicking the Caucasian kid, except for my friend and me. I immediately jumped in and started pushing people away. Once I finally reached him, I put my body in between him and everyone else while my friend stood in front me.

Immediately the African-American kids began to call me a traitor along with other derogatory comments. I wasn't worried about anyone trying to attack me, because I wasn't a small person by any means, and besides, my brother was the biggest guy in the school; everyone was already afraid of him. They also knew if they messed with me, they surely were going to have deal with my brother. I eventually got the kid to my car and took him home. The following day, one of the African-American kids who hit the kid several times asked me why I didn't stand behind them by jumping in and hitting the Caucasian kid. I replied, "It wasn't about color or standing behind my people, it was about doing the right thing, because the fight was unfair and uneven."

I then asked him, "How would you feel if you were fighting a Caucasian kid and five or six other Caucasian kids jumped on you?" He responded by saying, "That would be unfair." I replied, "I felt the same way when everybody jumped on the Caucasian kid and I'm sure he definitely felt the same way."

The moral to this incident is, when I saw that the Caucasian kid didn't have a fair chance, I felt that I had to do something. It didn't matter what color he was, because I simply saw him as an individual and I had to do the right thing. Many times, we get put in situations and we have to make the decision if we are going to be black men or men who happen to be black. Sometimes standing behind and supporting your own race is not always the best thing or the right thing.

However, the best thing and the right thing is to simply stand behind and support one another as a **human race**.

When human beings can view each other as individuals, only then will we begin to realize and understand that color has no right or wrong, because right is right and **wrong is wrong.**

I do realize and understand that racism and prejudice still exist. However, as men who happen to be black, white, or brown, we do not have to continue to add to the existing problem.

If we just simply view ourselves as men first, we can help make a difference and do our part in helping this world to become a better place to live. We don't have to adopt the mentality of racism and prejudice.

REALITY CHECK

As a human race, we must begin to be helpers, one to another, because helping or giving to someone really doesn't require much effort. We are so into ourselves, but the reality is the majority of us are a paycheck away from being broke or struggling. I believe that every so often, we should do a reality check by conducting a thorough re-evaluation of ourselves. At least five times a year, I will drive through the worst parts of Houston, looking at homes that are not fit to live in and should be condemned. The whole time, I'm thinking, how can a person live in something like that? And the reality is, someone is living there. As a man who happens to be black, I make it a point to see things like that because it helps to keep me humble and it also makes me appreciate what God has blessed me with, because the reality is, that could be me. It lets me know that poverty, conditions, and circumstances have no particular race, but exist in all races. So the next time you go out to eat and you see a homeless person holding a sign saying "I'll work for food" near the place you plan to eat at, stop and tell them to meet you there, and buy them something to eat.

If possible, sit and talk with that person, because he or she just might have a profound word that may help you in some way. If nothing else, it will help you to appreciate all that God has blessed you to have and be able to do.

The next Thanksgiving and Christmas dinner you have, don't throw your leftovers in the trash. Please package it up and take it to someone homeless who was not able to have Thanksgiving and Christmas dinner. It just may be your giving or words of encouragement that help that person get their life back on track, because the reality is, that could be you.

This upcoming Thanksgiving and Christmas, invite someone you know to dinner whose parents may be deceased, or they can't afford to go home, because the reality is, that could be you sitting at home alone next Thanksgiving or Christmas.

My point is this: showing a little love, concern, and consideration doesn't cost a thing and besides, it just may be the very thing that helps a person get their life jump-started again. The reality is, one day you may need someone to help you jump-start your life again. Under the circumstances, I'm sure it wouldn't matter to you whether that individual was black, white, green, or purple.

CHAPTER THREE

SELECTIVE PREJUDICE

As a human race, we all have what I call selective prejudice and racism, which means we pick and choose when we want to be prejudiced and racist. As a human race, many of us choose to be open to being exposed to different cultures and environments when it benefits us in some way, shape, form, or fashion. As a matter of fact, many of us are not as prejudiced and racist as we think we are, but many of us we feel like have to play the role or portray that persona in order to continue to be accepted by our social peers.

Just to validate my point, on occasion I like to eat soul food. There are three different soul food restaurants in Houston, Texas that I mainly go to, and they are all located in bad areas. While I'm there, I always notice the number of Caucasians eating there. Every time I have gone to any of the three restaurants, at least half of the people there are Caucasian, which I love to see, simply because it lets me know that they are open-minded enough to expose themselves to things of different culture.

As an ex-athlete, I've talked to several athletes, college and professional, who stated they really don't care for Caucasians, just as some Caucasians stated they don't care for African Americans. When I attend sporting events such as football and basketball games, I noticed at least 70 percent of the people in the stands are Caucasian and probably 70 percent of the athletes that they are paying to see are African Americans. As African Americans, we must stop and think that if all those Caucasians we not there filling up the stands and cheering you on, then you wouldn't be getting paid those huge salaries, because if you had to rely on African Americans to fill the stands to pay your salary, you would all be unemployed. As Caucasians, you must stop to think if all of those African Americans were not playing these sports, would there be entertainment for you to attend?

My point is this: We people choose to see color and be prejudiced and racist in some aspects of our lives, but choose to be color blind in other aspects of our lives, especially when it benefits them in some way. Being prejudiced and racist is a choice, just as not being prejudiced and racist is a choice. If we can support one another by eating each other's food and paying to see each other run up and down a football field and basketball court, then we can surely stand behind and support each other as a human race, and in every aspect of our lives, if we choose to do so.

A Different Kind of Color Blind

I constantly try to help friends and associates who view themselves as men who are prejudiced or racist, by trying to get them to have a different mentality, thought process, and mindset by seeing things from a different perspective and understand that all men who happen to be white are not devils or honkies and all men who happen to be black are not ghetto or niggers.

There were two men who happened to be white who wrote me a check for $10,000 and one for $5,000 when I had to start all over after my divorce. There was a man who happened to be white with two kids who gave me the key to his house and told me I was more than welcome to stay free for as long as I needed after my divorce.

There was a man who happened to be white who told my mother that she didn't have to worry about anything and gave her a key to his house after going through her divorce. There was a woman who happened to be white who helped me educate thousands of people with valuable information when I was rejected by at least five different radio stations that happened to be black.

So I have nothing but love for men and women who happen to be white, simply because I see them as just a man and a woman first. Please don't get me wrong; there were those of the black race who helped as well, but I used these points to show that all people who happen to be Caucasian are not devils.

In 1990 I moved to Austin, Texas after graduating from college. I had a full-time job as a juvenile probation officer, but decided to work a part-time job. I mentioned to my brother that I was interested in getting a part-time job. At the time, my brother was already working a part-time job as a referee in Westlake Hills. He told me that he was the only referee and he could use some help. He told me that the parents of Westlake Hills put together a basketball league for children who did not make the basketball team at their schools. He also told me that we would be the only African Americans in the whole gym. My immediate thought was to say no, simply because I was told by several African Americans when I first moved to Austin that Westlake Hills was an all-white, very upscale community that didn't care for African Americans. I eventually said yes, because my brother needed the help. We worked from 8:00 AM to 6:00 PM, with a one-hour break from noon to 1:00 PM. I will never forget the first weekend I worked, during our one-hour break at approximately 12:15, a Caucasian gentleman walked up to my brother and me with two large bags. He said, "I brought you some barbeque for lunch and since I didn't know what you like, I just bought a little bit of everything." Every weekend, Mr. Gressett brought us lunch. Every weekend, different parents would invite my brother and me to their home for Sunday dinner, which we accepted. By the end of the season, my brother and I had built such an awesome rapport with the parents and their children, the parents wanted to pay my brother and me to open a summer camp for their children during the summer. I am still friends with many of them today. I am sure there are some people who live in Westlake Hills who are prejudiced and racist. But on the other hand, I know for a fact, there are some very nice people who live in Westlake Hills, because my brother and I had the opportunity to meet and have dinner with many of them.

That summer, I learned a lifelong lesson. I learned that it is okay to listen to others and take advice, but it is always better to be open to taking the time to find out some things for yourself.

As a human race, we must learn that sometimes people give us incorrect information. We must be careful who we listen to, because they just may be the same person who had a bad encounter with someone of a different race, and they are holding the entire race responsible for what one or two have done.

As a man who happens to be black, I made a promise to myself to make it a point to speak to someone of a different race throughout the day every day. As a human race, we have no idea what others have gone through to cause them to think the way they think, say the things they say, or do the things they do. I do know one thing for sure: Struggles, hurt, pain, disappointment, poverty, and anything else that may affect someone's life in a negative manner is not only limited to the African-American race, but it exists in all races. The reality is, we will always have encounters (good and bad) with people of the same race and people of a different race, but we shouldn't let it divide us as a human race.

We should all make it point to speak to someone of a different race throughout the day every day, because that may be the same person who had a bad encounter with another African American and now they view all African Americans the same. I make it a point to speak, because by my speaking to that individual and their speaking back, in my mind, just for that very moment, they see me as a man who just happens to be black.

I also believe if I speak to someone of a different race every day by simply saying hello, that may be the same person who I begin to help change their mentality who thinks that all African Americans are niggas, thugs, drug dealers, and hoodlums.

I also make it a point to speak because he or she may be the president, vice president, or executive of a company who is looking for a specific person who has a certain personality and qualities, and has the ability or authority to hire.

There have been several times that I have spoken to someone of a different race and eventually engaged in a conversation and ended up getting offered a job. Although I didn't accept, several friends have reaped the benefits because I referred them to the individual and they ended up getting the job.

As a race, we must understand that speaking to someone by simply saying *hello* may open the door of opportunity for you, family members, or friends. But most importantly, it will help break down racial barriers because you just may be helping someone get past a fear or stereotype that has also held them in bondage for years, or maybe all their lives.

As a human race, we must continue to work on getting to a point in our lives when we realize that being nice and speaking to one another doesn't cost a thing.

LENDING A HELPING HAND

For whatever reason, many African Americans continue to dwell and live in the past. As a race, we must realize and understand that we now live in the present, and if you continue to live in the past, you will always be two steps behind. I've had many African Americans ask me "Do you like white people?" My response to that was, "I love people who happen to be white." I also responded by saying "I've had more people who happen to be white help me than people from my own race."

As a race, we have to come to the reality and conclusion that the Caucasian race of today had nothing to do with how their parents and foreparents treated our parents and foreparents.

As a man who happens to be black, I refuse to hold men and women of today, who happen to be white, responsible for something that they had nothing to do with, and neither should you.

To let the truth be known, as African Americans, many of us should take a long, hard look in the mirror and re-evaluate ourselves as individuals. Many of us try to condemn and talk about other races, especially the Caucasian race, when we as a race, in my opinion, are the most prejudiced race. We are not only prejudiced against other races, but we are also prejudiced, jealous, and envious of our own race.

In 1991, I wrote a book called *Secret Information to Effectively Master Negotiating Automobile Prices* because I was tired of seeing consumers get cheated and taken advantage of, especially African Americans and Hispanics.

Before I started trying to promote my book, I remember my mother telling me not to get disappointed and discouraged if I didn't get any assistance and support from African Americans who have the power, ability, and authority to help me get this valuable information to the public.

The book contained very valuable information that would definitely educate the consumer, because it gave them detailed information that only the automobile dealerships had access to. Since the African-American and Hispanic races were being affected the most, I decided to go to the number-one African-American radio station in Austin at that time, to get them to help me educate the African-American public and whoever else listened to that particular station.

After meeting with a man who happen to be black, he told me that the book was excellent and he wanted to do a live interview with me to get this valuable information to the public. He told me to call him the following week and he would give me a time and date for the interview. When the time came, I called him as instructed.

After several attempts, I noticed that he wouldn't return my call. I consistently called and left messages for an entire week, with still no return call. I eventually talked to a young lady working there who I knew personally, who just happened to be black . I talked to her briefly and asked her to relay a message for me. I waited for two days, but still no call.

I eventually became frustrated, because now I had no way to help educate consumers with valuable information that I knew they would want and need.

Two weeks later, I happened to see the young lady who worked there, at the mall. I asked her why the gentleman never called me back, and she told that the gentleman said "he was not going to contribute to helping me get rich." Little did the gentleman know that I had planned on donating half of the proceeds that I made from the book back to the radio station, because they constantly struggled financially.

I continued trying to promote my book with other African-American radio stations within the city, but no one helped.

I even went to other cities with prominent, well-known African-American radio stations, without success. After dealing with five different African-American radio stations, I decided it was time to move on and try something different. I then went to the number-one Caucasian radio station, but at the time, the woman I needed to talk to wasn't there. I left a copy of the book and a detailed note introducing myself and what I was trying to do.

Approximately four hours later, a woman who happened to white called me, stating that the book was awesome and she needed to get this valuable information to the public. One week later, I was at the radio station, doing a thirty-minute live interview with her.

After the interview, she called her friend who worked at the number-two Caucasian radio station and told her what happened, and she also needed to interview me because I had information that the public needed to know. One week later, I was doing a thirty-minute live interview. She called another friend, and I eventually ended up doing interviews with five different Caucasian radio stations.

Shortly thereafter, I received a call from Channel 2 television station, asking me would I like to be on television regarding my book, and of course I accepted. Around 2 PM that same day, I received a phone call from the gentleman who never returned my call, stating that he saw me on television and offering congratulations. He then asked me if I would do an interview with him.

In all honesty, my initial and immediate thought was to say no, because I went to him first, and now that I had gotten all this exposure, he wanted to interview me. However, I did do the interview, because I realized that I had to remove my personal feelings. It wasn't about me, it was about me helping and educating thousands of people who needed this valuable information.

I will admit, I was very disappointed and mad with the African-American radio stations, simply because they had the power and authority to help thousands of people, especially African Americans. But because of jealousy, envy, or whatever reason toward me, they failed and neglected to help the very people who were supporting them and their radio stations.

I wasn't mad with the entire African-American race because, first of all, they couldn't buy or support something that they knew nothing about. Secondly, I couldn't hold the entire African-American race responsible for what one or two have done.

As a race, oftentimes we continue to hold each other back by having a crab-in-the-bucket mentality. If you put crabs in a bucket and one of them reaches the top, the others will always pull it back down. We must get to the point in our lives where we stand behind one another and support those who strive to better themselves and become successful. But for whatever reason, many African Americans do not like to see other African Americans succeed or become successful.

EXPERIENCING DIFFERENT CULTURES

As a race, many times we look forward to seeing others fall, fail, and hit rock bottom. This is why it is so important that we as a race be open to being exposed to different cultures and environments. We can definitely learn a lot from other races about sticking together, standing behind each other, and helping each other get to the next level by being supportive and lending a helping hand when possible.

Oftentimes, African Americans talk about Caucasians, Hispanics, Chinese, and other races, when we should be trying to emulate and adopt their mentality. One thing is for sure: They all know how to stick together, stand behind each other, and support one another, and that's why a lot of them are successful.

I honestly and wholeheartedly believe that we will become more successful as a race, once we realize and understand that sticking together, standing behind each other, being supportive of one another, and lending a helping hand has no color, limits, or boundaries to any particular race.

I choose to live in the present and take full advantage of opportunities and all that life has to offer. As a race, if we continue to hold men and women who happen to be white, responsible for something they had nothing to do with, then many of us will never reach our full potential. We fail to realize that we close the doors to potential opportunities.

The reality is, many African Americans are still in bondage and continue to hold themselves captive because of their mentality, thought process and mindset, without even realizing it. I am eternally grateful, thankful, and appreciative for the struggles that my parents and foreparents went through, because I now have the opportunity to become whatever I choose to become.

No Color?

Louis Bolden is my biological father, who happens to be black. However, I have three other fathers who call me and treat me as their son, and they just happen to be white. When I was ten years old, it was Jimmy Little, a man who happened to be white, who told me "Never look at yourself as a black man, but see yourself as a man first and you can accomplish anything you want to." Through the actions of many men and women who happened to be white, I have learned that love has no color. Only racism, prejudice, and hate know color.

I have come to the conclusion that as adults, we can all learn from small children. I remember one day, my brother and I had decided to take my five-year-old niece to the park to feed the ducks and the fish. At the time we walked through the park, it happened to be empty with no other kids around.

After approximately ten minutes, a young girl and her mother, who happened to be white, showed up. Needless to say, the ducks and fish were now out of luck, because it was now playtime for my niece, since she now had a playmate. The two girls approached one another and immediately began to play.

As I sat at the end of the bench watching them play, my heart was filled with joy and my eyes were filled with tears. What I saw was two human beings just simply playing together, running together, holding hands together, and laughing together without a care in the world, as if they had been friends since birth.

After two hours had gone by, it began to get dark, so it was time to go home. The two girls said their goodbyes and went their separate ways. As we were walking home, my niece turned to me and said, "That's my new friend."

At that very moment, I realized that as adults, many of us need to go back to a childhood mentality and innocence, when our minds were free from color, racism, and prejudice. It is clearly evident that racism and prejudice is not instinctive, it is a learned behavior.

In talking to hundreds of men who consider themselves as black men, who stated that they didn't care for people who happen to be white, I asked this question: **What if you made it to heaven on Judgment Day, and when you got there, you found out that Jesus just happened to be white, would you still want to be in heaven?** To no surprise, everyone stated they would still go to heaven. If so many are willing to adopt that mentality, then why can't we adopt that same mentality now, because it is going to take that mentality to get into heaven.

The reality is, we do have the ability to control our thought process and mindset. However, we choose to be selective instead, which means we control our thought process and mindset when we choose to do so, or when it benefits us, instead of utilizing it at all times.

To validate my point, I had an opportunity to interview several men who viewed themselves as a black man, who stated they really didn't care for people who happen to be white, although they never really had a negative encounter or bad experience with one. Some had parents who had divorced; eventually, their mothers married men who happen to be white who already had kids.

They now had brothers and sisters who happened to be white. After living in the same household, they eventually became familiar and comfortable with one another.

I then asked the question, when you went places together and you came across friends, how did you introduce your stepbrother or stepsister? They all stated they introduced him or her as their brother or stepbrother, and sister or stepsister. My point is this: They didn't introduce them as "my white brother" or "white sister," they introduced them as "my brother or sister," which means they didn't see color, they simply saw them as a man or woman who became their brother or sister. When you view an individual as just a man or woman first, with that comes a certain level of respect toward one another.

When you see color first, everything automatically becomes distorted, because you then begin to differentiate and associate equality.

After months of constant research and conducting numerous interviews, I found that the majority of people who view themselves as a black man, seem to always feel like they have to live up to the expectations of being black. In there efforts to prove their blackness, many refuse to expose themselves to different environments and cultures. An extremely high majority only involved themselves in things of black culture, when the truth of the matter is, all they have to do is live up to the expectations of just simply being a man who happens to be black.

THE WRONG EXPECTATIONS

I remember attending a mandatory meeting in Austin, Texas with approximately fifty people. The instructor gave instructions for everyone to introduce themselves by giving their name, title or position, the particular dealership they were employed with, and how long they had been in the business. Also attending the meeting was an associate I knew who happened to be extremely pro-black and definitely viewed himself as a black man. Everyone in the meeting did as they were asked by giving the necessary information as instructed. When they got to the gentleman who viewed himself as a black man, he gave his name, how long he had been in the business, and then stated he was from "the dog pound." Immediately, the majority of the class turned toward the gentleman, trying to understand what "the dog pound" meant.

Shortly thereafter, another gentleman from the same department, who happened to be black, clarified what the "the dog pound" meant, by saying "He works in the used car department."

After the meeting, I approached the gentleman and asked him, "What made you say what you said and why did you say it?" He stated that he was supporting his people and wanted everybody to know that he was a black man. I immediately responded by saying, "What does being a black man have to do with this meeting that we are attending?" He had no answer.

It is a proven fact that an extremely high majority of men who view themselves as a black man, always feel like they have to prove and let people know that they are black at all times.

I find it difficult to understand why men who view themselves as a black man do not want people to see them as simply a man first. Instead, everything they do has to be associated with our culture and race.

The majority of men who view themselves as a black man have mentally incorporated our race, culture, and past in their daily vocabulary, conversation, and also in every aspect of their lives.

At that point, you now have a one-track mind and you are no longer open to being exposed to anything else outside of what you believe or consider to be of black culture. You are also in bondage, but most importantly, you have shut the door to opportunities of success.

I also noticed that the majority of men who view themselves as a black man constantly complain about not having chances or opportunities, when in reality, we limit our own chances and opportunities to achieve and reach our full potential due to our mentality, thought process, mindset, lack of education, and lack of having a open mind to different cultures and environments.

For whatever reason, many African Americans feel like they have to be defined by their race, when in actuality, we should all be defined by our individuality.

We have to come the reality, understanding, and conclusion that we are one race, and before we were defined by our color, we were the human race.

It is important that we understand that our parents and foreparents lived during a time when they didn't have very many choices or opportunities, because the society they lived in controlled and dictated their mentality, thought process, and mindset.

It is equally important we understand that we now have choices and opportunities, so there is no reason for our generation to continue to allow society to dictate, determine, define, or control our thought process, mindset, or destiny.

As men, we must have enough confidence in ourselves to know that we have the ability, power, and authority to dictate, determine, define, and control our own destiny as an individual.

CHAPTER FOUR

It is a reality and a true fact that however you view yourself, it becomes a part of you and how you live every aspect of your life. If you view yourself as a thug, then you will act and carry yourself in a thuggish manner. If you view yourself as someone with class, one who is professional, then you will act and carry yourself in a classy and professional manner. It is also a fact that the majority of men who view themselves as a black man normally have a negative view and attitude on life in general.

While listening and conversing with numerous men who view themselves as a black man or nigga, I noticed that they would constantly ridicule and tear down those who view themselves as a man who happens to be black, who were successful or striving to be successful, for no reason at all. It was very disheartening because I realized that racism, prejudice, jealousy, and envy lie within our race. It was clearly evident that men who view themselves as a black man had to hold someone responsible for their own personal failures and prejudice, and who better to choose than their own and the Caucasian race. I couldn't understand how anyone could hold someone else responsible for the wrong choices that they made in their own lives.

On several occasions, I have personally witnessed men who consider themselves a black man, belittle and tear down men who view themselves as a man who happens to be black for no reason at all.

Change Brings about Change

I have a friend that I have known for several years, who is educated, classy, well-spoken, professional, and successful, who is engaged to an absolutely beautiful woman. He owns an insurance agency and he was trying to expand his business by getting more clients. He had recently opened up an office around the corner from the dealership where I work.

In an effort to help my friend get started, I told him to come by the office with his business cards, and I would introduce him to every salesman at the dealership. After introducing him to everyone who worked in the new car department, I decided to also introduce him to every salesman who worked in the used car department as well. I eventually got around to introducing him to a gentleman who views himself as a black man and is definitely pro-black. After a brief introduction and short conversation that lasted no longer than two minutes, we moved on to others. In less than thirty minutes, I received a phone call from two different people, stating that the salesman had made the comment that my friend was gay, along with other derogatory comments. I was very disturbed and disappointed in the fact that he felt the need to judge, and tore down a man he didn't even know. I immediately begin to wonder why he would judge and make derogatory comments about a man who is educated, intelligent, well-spoken, and successful, who had never said or done anything to him.

Instead of looking at my friend as a man who is trying to better himself and become more successful, he chose to be negative and tear down a God-fearing, hard-working, intelligent man who happened to be black, for no reason at all. As a matter of fact, this is not the first time that he has made negative and derogatory comments toward educated, intelligent, and successful men who just happen to be black.

If you view yourself as a black man, instead of viewing yourself as a man first, that is your choice. Being ignorant as opposed to being educated is also a choice.

As a race, we have to get to a point in our lives where we understand that we do have choices. Most importantly, we must understand that our mentality, thought process, mindset, and the choices we make affect and determine the outcome and destiny of our lives.

That statement became a reality for an associate I knew when he finally realized and came to the conclusion that he could become anything he wanted to become once he changed his mentality, thought process, and mindset. James is a man I have known for approximately twenty-five years who happens to be black. He had a cousin named Kenneth, who everyone knew would one day become successful.

As kids growing up together, whenever you saw James, you saw Kenneth. As they got older, they began to develop their own individuality. James decided to hang out with other kids who skipped school, stole from others, and hung out on the street corners. Kenneth decided to occupy his time by playing sports and working whenever he had free time. After graduating from high school, James stayed in our hometown, working different jobs, but nothing consistent.

Kenneth went to college, eventually graduating, and later became an executive for a marketing company.

Every now and then, Kenneth would return to our hometown to visit his parents. Sometimes James would go to visit Kenneth, who lived in an upscale neighborhood. James owned a car that was nine years old, that had a stereo system that you could hear from miles away.

Kenneth drove a new BMW, but also had a second car that was only two years old. Since we were all from the same hometown, I would also go home periodically to visit my mother and my son. In the summer of 2001, I went home to visit my mother and son, and happened to run into Kenneth, who was also there visiting his parents. During our conversation, I asked about James. Kenneth told me he was fine but he didn't talk to James often, because James was mad at him. He elaborated by telling me that James used to come visit him all the time. However, when James would come to visit, he would drive through the neighborhood with his music playing very loud.

He went on to tell me that James would do this every time he came to visit. He said he explained to James time and time again that playing loud music was not allowed in that particular neighborhood. In addition, he also explained to James that it was very rude, disrespectful, and inconsiderate to the other neighbors who lived there. He stated that eventually, he had to tell James that if he didn't stop, he would no longer invite him to his house to visit. He then said that James got mad and has not been back to visit since. We continued to talk for a brief moment and eventually said our goodbyes and went our separate ways.

The following day, I went to visit an old friend who was having a barbeque. As I was talking to a high school classmate, someone tapped me on my shoulder, and it happened to be James. We immediately shook hands and began to talk about the past, present, and future.

Eventually, he got around to mentioning Kenneth. He started out by saying, "I don't fool with my cousin Kenneth because he thinks he's better than everybody else." I then asked the question, "Why do you say that and what makes you think that?" I had to ask, because I knew Kenneth personally and that wasn't his personality or character. For some reason, I felt there was more to this story than what James was willing to tell or admit. He replied, "Every time he comes home, he has to ride by everybody's house, trying to show off his new BMW." He also stated, "Kenneth always wears expensive clothes and lives in a white neighborhood, and he's the only black living there."

At that point, I really didn't care to hear much more, but I had to listen in order to get a clear understanding of James's thought process and mindset. He finally told me about the incidents that occurred when he went to visit Kenneth, and to no surprise, it happened just as Kenneth said it did. I told James that I also lived in an upscale neighborhood and it didn't matter to me who lived there, because that just happened to be the neighborhood I chose to live in.

I expressed my opinion by explaining to James that I would not allow or appreciate any family member or friend coming to my neighborhood to visit me, playing loud music and disturbing the privacy of other neighbors. I told James that it had nothing to do with me or Kenneth thinking we were better than anyone else; it was simply a matter of respect and consideration for other people who lived in the neighborhood.

I also told James that I drive a BMW. I can afford it, that's the car that I chose to buy, and once again, that doesn't mean that I think I am better than anyone else.

I expressed to James that if Kenneth or I thought we were better than everyone else, we would come to town see our parents and not bother trying to talk to anyone else. I then asked James, "Is there a possibility that you are jealous and envious of Kenneth because he is successful and you're not?" I told James that becoming successful is a choice, just as not becoming successful is a choice, so don't be jealous, envious, or mad at Kenneth because he chose to become successful.

As a race, we also have to understand that no one has any idea what a person had to endure and encounter to become successful, especially as a man who happens to be black. I explained to James that since he was not trying to be promoted on his job, he was not a potential threat to anyone, so therefore, he doesn't have to go through anything, because he is content with making $12 per hour.

I explained to him that Kenneth and I had to more than likely go through three times more than he did to get to where we are now. So if anything, you should be proud of Kenneth and ask him what you can do to become successful as well. As a race, we have to remember there was a time when we couldn't drive a BMW or a Mercedes. There was also a time when we couldn't live in the upscale neighborhoods, because we weren't allowed, and we surely couldn't afford it. We now have choices and opportunities, however; we just have to make the right choice and take advantage of the opportunities.

I told James to keep in mind that Kenneth may be in a position to help him, but he has to be willing to put forth the effort to become successful, and not expect anything to be given to him for free.

I then asked James what was his favorite type of car, and he answered Mercedes-Benz. I commented by saying, "Why don't you go buy one?" He replied, "I can't afford it." I then asked, "If you made enough money on your job and could afford the payment, would you buy one?" Of course he said yes.

I then asked him, "If you made over $80,000 a year and had the opportunity to buy a house, what area would you choose?" and he stated "Bluff View area," which happens to be an upscale, predominantly white neighborhood. I tried to encourage James by telling him that he could buy that Mercedes that he wanted to drive and he could buy that house that he wanted to live in. However, he had to stop seeing himself as a black man and a nigga, and see himself as simply a man first, who happens to be black, because success has no color, boundaries, or limits.

I ended the conversation by telling James that he has the power, ability, and authority to control his own destiny by changing his mentality, thought process, and mindset, and seeing himself as simply a man first, who happens to be black.

James is now driving a Mercedes-Benz, lives in a $200,000 home in an upscale neighborhood, and is currently working for an engineering firm. James is one of many who finally figured out that he could control his own destiny by changing his mentality, thought process, and mindset.

He also utilized and took advantage of the opportunities and choices that are available to millions of other African Americans, whom I hope will make the decision that James made.

CHAPTER FIVE

As men who happen to be black, it is very important that we view ourselves as men first. However, it is equally important we understand that it is more to being a man than just viewing ourselves as men. We must keep in mind that just because many of us have become successful, we cannot become complacent. Many of us have children, and that means we have additional responsibilities.

What Are We Teaching Our Children?

As a race, we must realize and understand that the things we instill in our children will have a major impact on their morals, values, mentality, mindset, thought process, and destiny in life. It is imperative that we understand that we have a responsibility to ourselves and our children, to make sure we give them every opportunity to succeed and become successful men who happen to be black.

However, many African-Americans focus less on being fathers and more on helping our children be cool, popular, and accepted into a social group. As a race, we must realize and understand that what we sometimes think is cool or the "in-thing" is not always the best thing or the right thing.

In many ways, as a race we have regressed instead of progressed in certain areas. As responsible men who happen to be black, we must take pride in setting examples and being role models for our children.

As a race, we continue to do our own children a disservice and injustice by allowing them to follow fads and cool trends that stereotype them as disrespectful.

I personally find it embarrassing and a disgrace to our race when our children dress in meaningless and negative ways. In my opinion, it has no meaning and serves absolutely no purpose, and there is nothing positive about it. Such behavior it is an insult to our foreparents, who went through far too many struggles in order for us to have choices, opportunities, and a better life. There is absolutely no reason for us to allow our children to do certain things such as the following:

Walk around in public with baggy pants sagging past their butts with their underwear showing. I am sure I speak for many others by saying we don't care to see your child's underwear in public.

Walk around in public with afros, ponytails, cornrows, and tattoos.

Walk around with earrings in both ears. Earrings were made for women to wear, not men.

Walk around in public with gold and silver teeth in their mouth that weren't recommended by a dentist.

In the year 2000, I remember going home to visit my son, who was fourteen years old at the time. When I got to his house, he greeted me at the door, full of excitement. As we turned to go into the house, I noticed he had an earring in his ear, his hat was turned to the side and his pants were sagging past his butt and I could see his underwear.

I immediately asked two questions and then gave two demands. I asked him when did he get the earring and where did he think he was going with those pants hanging off his butt with his underwear showing? I then told my son that he would not wear an earring, and he surely wasn't going anywhere with me, dressed like that. I told him to put on some pants that fit properly, and of course, he didn't like it, but he knew better than to say anything. As we were walking to my car to go get something to eat, I began to explain to him that just because the majority of other kids are wearing earrings and wearing saggy pants, that doesn't make it right.

I also explained to him that it is my responsibility as a father to make sure that I supply him with the right tools and ammunition to have a fair chance to succeed and become successful. I told him that it was my job to instill in him the correct morals and values. I felt as a father, I had to be a man by letting him know that his appearance determines how the public views him. As a teenager, I thought to myself many times that my parents did not know what they were talking about, and they were just being mean.

As a race, we complain and talk about being harassed, but oftentimes we put ourselves in situations that we really don't have to be in. Even to this day, my mother often tells me "Don't give anyone any ammunition to use against you and don't put yourself in a situation you don't have to be in, because it can take two minutes to get into, but cost you a lifetime to get out of."

In an effort to be the best father I can be, I realized that sometimes, children don't understand why we, as parents, make the decisions we make.

As a responsible father, I wanted my son to see that when you look a certain way and dress a certain way, the public views you a certain way. By this time, a friend of his happened to show up dressed the same way, an earring, saggy pants and a doo-rag on his head. At that I point, I decided to give my son and his friend a life lesson that would possibly help them for the rest of their lives.

I told my son to go put in his earring and put on his saggy pants. I drove my son and his friend to two different malls that had security officers. I told my son and his friend to walk by the security officer and act as if they were looking around for something, but nothing in particular. They did as I told them, while I stood back and watched. As they walked through different departments, the security officer followed them from a distance, everywhere they went. After approximately fifteen minutes, I signaled for them to come out.

As we left the mall, they immediately began to talk about being followed by the security officer; I never said a word. I then took them to a different mall and told them to do the same thing.

To no surprise, the security officer followed them from a distance everywhere they went. Again they immediately engaged in conversation about being followed by the security officers.

I drove my son and his friend back home and told them to take out their earrings, take off the doo-rag and the hat, and put on a nice shirt and some nice pants. I drove back to the same two malls and had them to go to the same department store and do the same thing they did the first time we came.

As I stood back and watched, they walked by the same security officer. He spoke to them, walked to the other side of the store, and never once did he follow them. As we got in the car and drove away, they began to talk about the results in amazement. We drove to the second mall and went to the same department store, and again, the same security officer was there.

As they walked toward the officer, there happened to be another group of kids entering the store who were dressed with the baggy pants, twisted hats, and some with gold teeth. The security officer looked at my son and his friend and immediately began to follow the other group of kids from a distance. After leaving the mall, they again engaged in conversation, **absolutely astounded by the results by just simply changing their appearance.**

At that point I found it necessary to tell them about two incidents that would validate that one's appearance determines how society views an individual. I begin to tell them about James Green, who was African-American gentleman who sold newspapers on the side of the road. Every Sunday after church, I would stop and get a newspaper from James. James and I would always laugh and joke about him needing to shave, get a haircut, and start going back to church. James always dressed in old, dingy clothes and tennis shoes. Approximately two months later, I stopped to get my newspaper from James as usual. However, I noticed James had on a suit, his hair was cut, and he had shaved. We laughed and joked, of course, but I had to ask James why he was wearing a suit. He told me that he had decided to go to church before coming to work. I told him that I was proud of him and I would be praying for him. Before leaving, for whatever reason, I asked James how business was, and he told me that it had been his best day ever. I said goodbye and I went on my way. I continued to stop and get my newspaper every Sunday, but I noticed James continued to wear suits in the 100-degree summer heat. I figured he was still going to church, but I also thought that he should consider changing into something more comfortable because of the heat.

After three weeks had gone by, I asked James why he didn't change clothes instead of wearing his suit in the heat. He told me that he gets paid by the number of papers that he sells, and since he shaved, cut his hair, and worn a suit to go to church three weeks ago, his sales have gone up tremendously. He also told me that more Caucasians were stopping to buy newspapers, and he was even getting more tips, so he didn't mind being hot, because he was making more money. Approximately four months later, James told me that it would be the last Sunday for him selling me my newspapers, because a Caucasian gentleman offered him a job working at an apartment complex, making double the money. I didn't ask many questions, but I did congratulate him and tell him that I was happy for him, and make sure he continues to go to church. It goes to show that an individual's appearance does matter, because it even changed the life of a man who sold newspapers on the side of the road. The reality is, your appearance determines how society views you, but most importantly, it will determine the number of people in society who are willing to associate with you in some shape, form, or fashion.

I then told them about a friend whose son was harassed then searched by mall security because of his appearance. She told me that just because her son had on baggy pants and his hat turned backwards, it doesn't mean that he's a thug or a gang member. She said that the officer had accused her son of trying to steal.

I actually know her son, and he happens to be a good kid. I don't know if he tried to steal, because I wasn't there. However, there are two sides to every story. If the security officer did accuse him of trying to steal without seeing him make the attempt to steal, then he was definitely in the wrong.

However, I did tell my friend that whole situation could have more than likely been avoided if she had not allowed her son to wear pants hanging off his butt, and his hat on backwards. I explained to her when police officers see kids with saggy pants, earrings, gold teeth, doo-rags, and hats, they associate that with being a hoodlum, gang member, or a thug. Granted, it's not fair that law enforcement officers or anybody else judge or assume that all kids who wear baggy pants, gold teeth, and hats are thugs, gang members, or hoodlums.

Life is seldom fair. We can't change the prejudice and the attitudes of other people; we can change their attitudes by not living up to their prejudice.

As responsible parents, we must also be aware, realistic, and keep in mind that many kids who do dress in that manner are gang members, hoodlums, and thugs.

I would also like to say, in defense of law enforcement, that we have no earthly idea what they go through every day. They put their lives on the line for us by dealing with gang members, hoodlums, thugs, and everything else, every day, and many of us do not appreciate it.

The reality is this: As long as we allow our children to dress in that manner, they will always to be viewed as thugs, gang members, and hoodlums by society in general.

The Wrong Kind of Support

As a race, we continue to contribute to many of our children's downfalls and failures in life. Oftentimes, we as parents stand behind and support our children when they do things, such as going to jail for stealing, selling drugs, and giving teachers a hard time because they have no discipline.

Many of our children's minds have become contaminated and corrupt due to the mentality, mindset, and thought process of the parents, because they stand behind and support their children when they know for a fact that their children are in the wrong. By doing this, you basically condone their lack of discipline and their misbehavior, so therefore, your children grow up thinking that they don't have to respect anyone or take responsibility for their own actions, simply because you support their lack of discipline, misbehavior, and wrongdoing.

I remember my mother telling me about an incident at her job. My mother works in a beauty supply store, but they sell a little bit of everything. She told that an African-American man came in the store with a child approximately five to seven years old. As the father was browsing, the child kept putting his hands on different items. Every time the child would put his hands on something, he would move it, knock it down, or knock it out of place.

My mother said she waited patiently for the father to tell the child to stop, which he never did. Eventually, my mother began to tell the child to leave things alone and stop putting his hands on everything.

She said she ended up having to tell the child several times. After numerous warnings, the father finally grabbed the child by the hand, gave my mother a dirty look, and said, "Come on, let's get out of this place."

This is one of probably a million examples of how children are now being raised. Based on his father's actions, this child's opportunities for success, through no fault of his own, have already diminished tremendously.

He has automatically become a prime candidate to be a statistic and will potentially be the same child who becomes an adult and the parents will wonder why he has no discipline, he's not responsible, and has no respect for people's property. Instead of giving him an opportunity to grow up and be a man who happens to be black, we end up paying more in taxes because he remains a black man who ultimately ends up behind bars, being raised by the prison system.

As African-American men, many make the typical and common mistake of trying to be the friend instead of the

father. Although it is very important that we be a friend, it is more important that we be a man, by being a father first.

As a juvenile probation officer for five years, I had the opportunity to experience firsthand the harsh reality of what a dysfunctional family really means. As a man who happens to be black:

I couldn't understand how a father could laugh and joke with his child as if nothing had ever happened during visitation hours after the child had just murdered someone forty-eight hours ago.

I couldn't understand why a father would go out with his child to the same club and party until three in the morning.

I couldn't understand why a father would sit and drink with his child until they both got drunk.

I couldn't understand why a father would smoke dope, sniff cocaine, shoot up with heroin, take speed and smoke crack with his child until they both passed out.

I couldn't understand why a father would help his child package up dope to be sold.

I couldn't understand how a father could sit at home and not work and allow his child to sell drugs to support the household.

I couldn't understand how a child could return to jail within forty-eight hours after being released by the judge to go home.

I couldn't understand why a father would have sex with his son's girlfriend while the son was incarcerated.

I couldn't understand why a father would go to his child's school and curse out the teacher because his child was misbehaving in class because he has no discipline.

I couldn't understand why a father would throw a chair across the courtroom and curse out the judge after his child wasn't released from jail, one week after robbing a convenience store clerk at gunpoint.

I
just
couldn't
understand!

But

after talking to the fathers, I could understand how and why those children became another statistic, just another black man who never had the opportunity to become a man who happens to be black.

As a race, we cannot continue to allow our children to become statistics. Many African Americans are now in prison, gangs, or dead because as men, many have failed to realize that just because something is cool or the "in-thing," it doesn't always mean that it's the best thing or the right thing. Life has no guarantees, but as men who happen to be black, it is imperative that we instill, mold, and nurture the mindset and thought process of our children. Many African Americans have failed as men and fathers, because we have allowed society to raise, mold, and control our children's thought process and mindset.

The solution is really simple; as responsible parents, it is our responsibility to make sure that we monitor, instill, mold, and nurture our children's thought process and mindset so that they do not become a statistic or viewed as anything other than boys or girls who happen to be black.

CHAPTER SIX

FIND THE POSITIVE IN A NEGATIVE SITUATION

As LONG AS WE LIVE, we will always have both good and bad encounters with people of different races. The reality is that racism, prejudice, jealousy, and envy are very much alive. That is why it is so important that we as men who happen to be black teach our children how to deal with these type of adversities, in the correct manner.

I remember traveling to Killeen, Texas to take care of some personal business for my mother. I was driving on Interstate 35 at approximately 73 to 75 mph, trying to make sure that I stay within 3 to 5 mph of the speed limit.

As I was approaching Belton, Texas, I was under the assumption that the speed limit was still 70 mph. I happened to look in my rear view mirror and I noticed that a state trooper was behind me with his lights on. I immediately pulled over to see why he was stopping me. He approached my car, introduced himself, and told me that I was driving 73 mph in a 55 mph zone. He then asked me for my driver's license and valid insurance card, and I complied with his request. I told the officer that I honestly thought the speed limit was 70 mph. I then told him that my brother was a sergeant for DPS in Houston, Texas and asked if he wouldn't mind just giving me a warning, since I honestly thought the speed limit was 70 mph. The officer stated that he really couldn't do that because I was too far over the limit allowed in order for him to give me a warning, which I knew was a lie. He went back his car, called in my information, and returned within minutes. He then told me to have my brother call him, but I noticed that he didn't leave a contact number where he could be reached. I asked him for a contact number and he stated that my brother would know how to get in contact with him. I knew something was wrong, because he didn't want to leave a contact number. I immediately thought to myself, why have my brother call if you already know that you are not going to dismiss the ticket anyway?

I also thought to myself, if you plan on dismissing the ticket, what would be the difference between dismissing the ticket now, as opposed to dismissing the ticket when my brother calls? Nevertheless, I decided not to debate with the officer, because of my respect for law enforcement. I signed the ticket and went on my way.

Upon returning to Houston, Texas, I immediately went to my brother's office, gave him the ticket, and explained what happened. Of course, my brother was a little upset, because the officer could have just written a warning citation. My brother called numerous times and left several messages, desperately trying to reach the officer, but he never returned the call. After trying to reach the officer for one week, my brother gave up, because it was obvious that he was not going to return the phone call. Two weeks later, my brother found out that the officer told another officer who knew my brother that he had stopped a black man driving a nice car with personalized plates whose brother is a sergeant in Houston, Texas.

He went on to say, "If he can afford to drive a nice car like that, he can surely afford to pay the ticket." I can agree that the officer was right about two things: I do drive a nice car and I can afford to pay the ticket, However, I am not a black man; I am a man who happens to be black.

Approximately six months later, I had to return to Killeen to finalize the previous business transaction. On my way back to Houston, I was driving through a small town outside of Milano, Texas. The road was extremely flat, so I could see miles ahead. After driving a few more minutes, I spotted a state trooper about a mile ahead of me.

As I got closer, I noticed he begin to slow down while pulling over to the shoulder. I wasn't speeding, but for some odd reason, I just had a feeling that he was going to stop me. As I drove past him, he immediately turned on his lights and I pulled over to the side of the road.

As he approached my car, he introduced himself and told me the reason he was pulling me over was because I didn't have a front license plate. I explained to the officer that it was a special plate made by BMW. I then told the officer that my brother was a sergeant for DPS in Houston, Texas and he told me that state troopers normally do not stop people for something like that, unless they don't have anything else better to do or they want to mess with someone in particular. The officer replied, "You are supposed to have a front license plate on your car." He then asked me for my driver's license and valid insurance card, which I produced at his request. He then went to his car to call in my information to see if I had any warrants. As I was looking in my rear view mirror, I noticed his partner walking to my car with a book in his hand, as he approached me from the passenger side of my car. He introduced himself and began to tell me about the law code regarding license plates.

I politely waited for the officer to finish and I replied by telling him, "I know by law you can write me a ticket." I told him my brother is a sergeant for DPS in Houston, Texas, and he told me that law enforcement normally does not stop people for something like this unless they have nothing better to do or they just feel like messing with someone in particular. The officer started laughing and replied, "You have a really nice car." I replied, "I know, and thank you very much." He then responded, "We don't get the opportunity to stop many people because this is a small town, so when we get a chance to stop someone, we do so."

By then, the other officer returned with my driver's license and insurance card and told me that he was just going to write me a warning, but I needed to get a front license plate when I got back to Houston. I told the officer "Thanks for the warning and have a nice day." When I returned to Houston, I immediately went to my brother's office. As I drove up, he happened to be standing outside. As I was getting out of my car, he immediately told me that my inspection sticker had been expired for two months. I told him about the incident and he began to laugh. He told me that he was amazed, because the officer was so focused and concerned about harassing me regarding my license plate, that he didn't even realize that my inspection sticker had been expired for two months. He went on to tell me that normally, when a law enforcement officer in a small town sees an African-American male driving an expensive car such as mine, they normally think it's a drug dealer, so they try to find a reason to stop them, hoping to find something.

Please know that I am not trying to belittle or disrespect law enforcement in any way, I am using this as a point of reference. I wholeheartedly have the utmost respect for law enforcement officers, because they put their lives on the line for people like myself every day.

As a race, we must learn to use other people's prejudice, jealousy, and envy as a motivation factor. What people intend for bad or evil, we must learn to somehow see the positive in it and turn it around for our good.

As a man who happens to be black, I make it a point to try to always see the positive in every situation and circumstance. The reason that most people are so negative is because it really doesn't require much energy to be negative. I also find that it doesn't matter how positive a person may be, people will always find something negative about them. For whatever reason, everyone seems to support people who are negative, but never support people who are positive. The problem is, being negative seems to be the norm, and it is accepted and embraced by society, so therefore it takes precedence over being positive. But the reality is, it's just as easy to be positive as it is to be negative, because being positive is a choice, just as being negative is a choice.

When I had those encounters with the law enforcement officers, it let me know that they saw me as successful, and moreover, it let me know that they were jealous and envious of my success.

The reality is, racism and prejudice are very much alive, and once you come to that realization, when you have an encounter, you don't allow yourself to be mentally consumed or involved, and revert back to your past. As long as you know that it still exists, you can't allow it to bother you. If you take their mentality, then you're right back where you started, a black man's mentality instead of the mentality of a man who happens to be black.

For the record, I still view those law enforcement officers as men who happen to be white, who just haven't been educated enough to know and understand that success has no color, limits, or boundaries.

What Will Our Children Choose?

It is a fact that our children are our future. One day, we will pass the torch, and our children will carry on our legacy. However, my concern is how will the next generation view themselves, as black men or men who happen to be black? Most importantly, will there be more black men or will there be more men who happen to be black? Whatever the case may be, **it is clearly evident that we need more men who happen to be black.** But from the looks of things, black men far outweigh men who happen to be black.

As a former athlete, I've had the fortunate opportunity to make a lot of friends, many of whom are now coaches at high schools and major universities.

As I continued my research, I wanted to get a better understanding of the mindset and thought process of the younger generation. I decided to ask several of my friends who are now coaches at high schools to ask male students and student athletes who are African

Americans, if they viewed themselves as a black man or a man who happens to be black. After gathering all the information, I found that 98 percent stated they were black men and only 2 percent inquired by asking the coaches to elaborate on what the difference was between the two.

This is our future!

I then asked two of my friends who are coaches at major universities, one being a basketball coach and the other a football coach, to do the same thing. The basketball team is 90 percent African Americans and the football team is 85 percent African Americans.

After talking to both coaches, every one of the athletes stated that they were black men. As I continued to interview other coaches, I decided to stop, because the results were all the same.

As a race, I will admit that we have come a long way; however, as you can see, we still have a long way to go. As African Americans, if we plan to have any type of decent future, somehow, someway, as a race of responsible men who happen to be black, we must pull together and get our children on the right track with their mentality, mindset, and thought process. As parents, we must understand that what we instill in our children now will not only determine their future, but ours as well.

As African Americans, we must instill certain things in our children, such as morals, values, respect, consideration, education, and so on. Most importantly, we must understand as parents that just because some of us didn't get an education, it doesn't mean that we shouldn't push our children to get an education. As responsible parents, we should constantly instill in our children education, morals, and values, instead of just standing by as our babies create babies and give up at ever succeeding.

As a successful man who happens to be black, I am not ashamed to say that neither one of my parents went to college. However, they constantly instilled morals and values, and pushed us to go to college and get an education, because they knew it would help open doors to success. I am proud to say that all four of us, their kids, have degrees. The problem with many African Americans is, since we as parents are not successful and didn't get an education, we don't push our children to become successful and get an education. So now you have a child who emulates the parents, who didn't do anything with their lives. The end result is, you now have a black man, who becomes another statistic, and never had an opportunity or chance to become a **man** who happens to be black.

Choosing Success

The reason that many African-American men are not successful is because they never think about being successful, so they don't see themselves as being successful. Therefore, they never become successful because they don't see success as an option. Many African-American men actually think that they do not have the knowledge or ability to become successful, simply because they have never been mentally equipped to even think that they can become successful. I honestly believe that many African-American men are ashamed, embarrassed, and disappointed in themselves as men and fathers. However, we must realize and understand that we still have a responsibility to ourselves and our children to make sure that we prepare them mentally by equipping and instilling in them that they can become successful.

As men, we must also understand that just because many of us have not become successful, that doesn't mean that we can't mentally equip our children for success.

As a race, it is time for us to stop using our conditions and circumstances as a crutch and an excuse. It is also time for us to stop justifying our poverty mentality by thinking that it is not remotely possible to become successful because of our conditions and circumstances. The reality is, it doesn't matter if you were born and raised in the slums of Houston or the ghettos of New York, you can overcome any condition, situation, or circumstance by changing your mentality, thought process, and mindset.

As men and fathers, many of us did not make the right choices and take advantage of the opportunities that were made possible by parents and foreparents. For many, the reality is, it may be too late; however, we can no longer be ashamed, embarrassed, or disappointed because of our lack of education, knowledge, downfalls, and failures.

As a race, as men, as fathers, we must now break the cycle and become responsible parents and make sure that we monitor, shape, mold, instill, and nurture our children's thought process and mindset, so that they will grow up and see themselves as men who can become successful, who just happen to be black.

As a race, this is definitely an area that we can improve on and learn from other races and cultures, especially Caucasian and Chinese. Many of them mentally equip their children to become successful at an early age, so when they become adults, all they know is success, because it has been instilled in their mental thought process and mindset.

It is a reality that many of them have the economical means, more so than African Americans. However, we cannot continue to use that as a crutch or an excuse, because we now have more opportunities than we ever thought we would have.

That is why it is so important that we as a race be open to being exposed to different cultures and environments. It is also important that we realize and understand that being successful and being exposed to different cultures and environments is not for any particular race, but open to all races.

There are many African-American men who are successful, and their parents did not have any education. My point is this: As a race, we must break the cycle and understand that it doesn't matter if many of us didn't get an education. However, we must now allow our children the opportunity that many of us never had or took advantage of.

CHAPTER SEVEN

A WOMAN'S PERSPECTIVE

TO FURTHER MY RESEARCH AND validate my perception of the African-American race, I decided to get several different opinions from a woman's perspective. I wanted to hear what women thought about African-American men who view themselves as black men, as opposed to men who view themselves as men who happen to be black.

Jessica, a woman who happens to be white writes, "In my opinion, I feel there is a distinction and it heavily relies on enculturation and socioeconomic status. How we are conditioned by our parents as children through our culture will determine how we act when we become adults. Our childhood produces who we are as adults, which means how we interact with our environment as children is how we determine ourselves as adults.

"I noticed that men who view themselves as being a black man have a total different outlook than a man who views himself as a man who happens to be black.

"I noticed that the majority of men who view themselves as being black, also refer to themselves and others around them as a 'nigga.' Many of them use this word very loosely and it is a part of their daily conversation and vocabulary. I also noticed that there is normally a difference in the character and demeanor.

"When I have an encounter (good or bad) with an African American, I can normally tell if I'm dealing with a man who views himself as a black man or a man who views himself as a man who happens to be black.

"I normally find the majority of men who view themselves as a black man to be very disrespectful, rude, loud, and use a lot of slang terminology. I also find that men who view themselves as black men have very little respect for themselves, women, or anybody else.

"I noticed that many grew up in single-parent homes and poverty or low-income households, leaving those parents struggling trying to make ends meet and provide for the family.

"Meanwhile, the children grow up unattended, with a lack of morals, values, and guidance, which leaves them having to fend for themselves, which leads to negative enculturation to set in and take its toll.

"Many times, I get approached by African-American men and I can normally tell the difference between the two by the way they dress and the way they carry themselves.

"After my encounter, I am right probably 99 percent of the time as far as distinguishing between the two. I noticed that many African Americans who view themselves as being black are not really open to doing much outside of their environment or culture.

"As far as those who view themselves as men who happen to be black, I find them to be more professional, well-spoken, well dressed, clean cut, educated, and polite. I find them to be very respectful toward women and others. I notice they normally have an excellent relationship with their mothers, which is very important to most women.

"I noticed that they seem to be open to doing more things outside of their environment and culture because they are confident in who they are as an individual.

"I also notice that men who view themselves as a man who happens to be black have a certain presence about themselves because they seem to see themselves as an equal. Sometimes they can even be very intimidating because they have such a strong presence of confidence and professionalism.

"To apply to the question, there is definitely a difference between a man who views himself as a black man and a man who views himself as a man who happens to be black. As a young woman who happens to be white, I have known black men I am highly comfortable with, and I have known black men who scare me significantly. The way in which I was approached and the commonalities between us made this distinction.

"Oddly enough, the men I am comfortable with, I do not label them as black. The men who scare me are always described as black. Is that right? I do not know, but I even apply this to my own race.

"At an onset of an approach, I do notice a man to be black as far as skin tone, simply because I use it as a physical judgment. Once again, is that right? I do not know, but I am sure everyone does it, especially in the presently physically obsessed society we all reside in. The difference can rely on how a black man presents himself.

"I noticed in the African-American culture, apparel seems to make a big difference in how many individuals view themselves. If he presents himself by wearing baggy jeans, big shirts, earrings, tattoos, gold teeth, and untied shoes, it leaves me thinking thug, hoodlum, or gang banger. If he presents himself by wearing a nice shirt with slacks, or a suit with a tie, he leaves me thinking he's a successful man who has himself together, and just happens to be black.

"Lastly, I feel that anyone can do or become whatever they choose to do or become; it just depends on how that individual views himself. As individuals, we can decide how to educate ourselves, present ourselves, and advance ourselves."

I wondered if other women would have similar reactions to my questions. I spoke with Erika, a CPA, who also happens to be white. She writes, "For a very long time, I have always known that there is a difference between a black man and a man who happens to be black.

"It is how one labels themselves and conducts their life. In my opinion, the 'black man' is a character that he creates in his own mind and then uses the media and his surrounding to portray and validate that image.

"I believe, though, unless he has the means and the money, he is never truly satisfied with the result of his present individuality. Thus, causing him to keep working on trying to reach for the unattainable because he doesn't realize it is just a facade he is creating.

"I normally view those who see themselves as a black man as the thug type, mainly because of their appearance and the manner in which they carry themselves. By me having two children in high school, I am exposed to seeing the different characteristics and behavior in the African-American race.

"When I see the baggy pants, earrings, tattoos, shoes untied, afros and gold teeth, I think of a thug or gang member.

"Although I see this in all races, it is more prevalent and taken more seriously in the African-American culture because it seems to define them as an individual and a race, for whatever reason.

"I noticed that men who view themselves as a black man seem to struggle with their identity, so therefore they do not see themselves as a man first, they see themselves as a black man. I also noticed that many men who view themselves as a black man are pro-black and it shows in their attitude, character, and actions.

"I noticed that men who view themselves as a black man seem to feel like they have to portray a hardcore persona, because they associate being tough with being a black man.

"I noticed that many men who view themselves as a black man are normally very negative, extremely loud, disrespectful, inconsiderate, and refer to themselves and others around them as a "nigga" as if it were their actual name. I also noticed that they seem to be extremely jealous and envious of successful men of their own race who are professional, clean cut, speak well, dress well, drive nice automobiles, and have nice homes in upscale neighborhoods.

"My opinion regarding a man who happens to be black is the type of man who I am attracted to. He is refined, professional, educated, successful, speaks well, dresses well, clean cut, well-rounded, diverse, and very confident in himself as a man and his individuality. He seems to be caring, open to being exposed to different cultures and environments, carries himself well, and cares about his appearance. He doesn't appear as if he has to prove anything to anyone because he knows he's a man.

"I noticed that they are always positive in general and very rarely say anything negative. I find that the majority of men who view themselves as a man who happens to be black are more family-oriented, stress education to their children, and always strive to become more successful.

"The reality is, an individual's appearance and how they carry themselves has no particular race attached to it. However, an individual's appearance and how they conduct themselves will determine how society views them as an individual."

It seems to be easier for people who happen to be white to view others as just people, without labeling their race. So I talked to a woman who happens to be black as well.

Denise, a director of operations who happens to be black writes: "When I was first asked to write about the differences between a black man and a man who happens to be black, I wasn't sure just what to write. Never before did I really distinguish the difference between a black man and a man who happens to be black until I met Mr. Brian Bolden.

"But in thinking about it and in various discussions, there is a marked difference in the behavior of both men.

"In my opinion, a black man feels the anger of our ancestors' history and the struggles [slavery] they had to bear and feel as though they bear the brunt of white society's disdain, carry a lot of anger for a history that is part of them but not as a whole.

"In carrying the anger and the resentment toward the white race, an image is created in our black men, that society owes them and that in order to be considered 'strong, black men,' they had to be hard and unyielding.

"The problem with this attitude is that it removes respect of oneself and the respect for others. You will find that a lot of the men who have this 'black man' mentality are angry, will use a lot of profanity, try to 'run game' to get ahead, and have little or no respect for themselves or other people.

"These are the men and the young men who hang on the street corners in the middle of the day, running the 'crap house' and in the clubs every weekend trying to push up on some unsuspecting target to get what he can.

"These are also the men who run out on their families, have several women pregnant, and the ones not taking care of their children. They are also the men who spend time in prison, blaming everyone, from their mother to society, for their plight.

"These are ones that fail to take responsibility for their own actions. There are those that will go out get a job to take care of their family, but complain about how they can't get ahead because of their color, or try to work the system to get ahead. They are the stereotypical 'black man' that gives the image of a drug dealer, loser, and lowlife that makes it harder for the black men who don't carry this mentality to get ahead.

"Now, the men who happen to be black usually seem to have a different mentality. They understand that though the color of their skin may be dark, it does not determine their success nor failure. They are the ones that believe if you work hard, respect yourself and others, and have integrity, that you may have the success and joys that life has to offer.

"These are the men who believe that it's what's on the inside that counts, not the color of their skin. They understand that it is how you treat others that will determine how far you go in life, what kind of life you will have, and how others will see you.

"Although it is unfortunate, there are people out there who will judge someone by the way they dress, how they speak and carry themselves, without taking the time to get know the individual inside. But the man who feels that he has to show off the 'black man' attitude will not get too far.

"The hip-hop fashion has and is continuing to degrade our young men. No one will take them seriously with their pants hanging down around their butt, large loose fitting T-shirts, and all that 'bling' hanging around their neck and the 'grill' in their mouth. The young men who 'happen to be black men' with their clean-cut looks, nice shoes and proper manners, are referred to as 'punks' or made fun of.

"When did proper manners and respect become a weakness or say that you weren't a strong man? When did it become uncool to speak proper English, or say please and thank you? But then again, how can you expect a man who does not respect himself to show respect to someone else?

"The 'black man' has to realize that he is better than what he sees on TV, reads in the latest *Vibe* or the nonsense in the latest rap video. Though we are not in the age of *Leave it to Beaver*, we need to remember how to conduct ourselves and move beyond the color of one's skin. Don't let the color of your skin define who you are; it's just a part. Be a man who just happens to be whatever color you are. Just be a man."

I am not at all amazed or surprised that these women came to the same conclusion I did.

EPILOGUE

As a man who happens to be black, I came to the reality years ago that as long as we are here on earth, we will be around men and women who happen to be black, white, brown, or whatever color they may be. Since it is inevitable that we cannot get away from one another, we might as well just all get along as a human race. I can promise it will make life so much easier for everyone, but most importantly, it will make this world a lot better place to live.

As a man who happens to be black, I decided to simply my life by trying to get along with everyone. I came to the conclusion long ago that no particular race is better than any other, because we are all a part of the human race.

The reality is, man was created equal, but it's unfortunate that we don't use what we were created with.

As a human race, we must stop believing everything we see and hear, and be willing and open to finding out about one another for ourselves. We must also be willing and open to giving each other the benefit of the doubt.

In doing so, we must be realistic in our thinking, because there will be many disappointments. The reality is, many will remain the same and not be willing or open to change or trying to make a difference. However, I believe there will be many who are willing and open to change and making a difference. Most importantly, remember this: whoever lets you down in your efforts to give them the benefit of the doubt, hold them and only them responsible, not the entire race to which he or she belongs.

As a race, we must stop tearing each other down, and learn to support and build each other up. For whatever reason, many African Americans take pride in tearing each other down. I would think that as much as our parents and foreparents have gone through, we would stick together more than any other race, But for some unknown reason, we are actually the most divided race that exists today.

As a race, we must realize and understand that we now have choices and opportunities that we never had in the past.

Most importantly, we must make the right choices and take full advantage of the opportunities, even if the odds seem high and the whole world seems to be against you as an individual, because it is still highly possible for African Americans as individuals to seek advancement and success.

As a race, we must realize and understand that our mentality, mindset, and thought process controls our destiny. We must also come to the reality and conclusion that we have all in the world to lose and nothing to gain by continuing to mentally live in our past.

As a race, many African Americans are unappreciative and ungrateful for the struggles of our parents and foreparents, because we continue to take things they have done and experienced for granted.

The reality is, many of us continue to disgrace and insult our parents and foreparents, because really and truly, we have no idea what they went through. Because of the struggles of our parents and foreparents, as a race we now have choices and opportunities that we otherwise would not have had if it had not been for them. As a man who happens to be black, I thank God I made the right choices and took advantage of the opportunities that were made possible by my parents and foreparents.

To show my gratitude, I therefore deemed it necessary out of respect and consideration, to end this book where it all began, with my parents and foreparents:

1. Who chopped cotton for 50 cents a day, but now I sleep on nice fluffy pillows filled with cotton.

2. Who stood in the line at the grocery store, and when white people came in, they had to step back or get out of line and let the white people get in front of them. But now I can go to the grocery store, buy whatever I want, and not have to worry about having to get out of line to let Caucasians get in front of me.

3. Who had to go to the back door of eating places to pick up their food. But now I can walk through the front door with my head held high, order from the menu, and eat with all races.

4. Who had to drink from a fountain that said "colored only." But now I can drink from any fountain without having to look at a sign saying "colored only."

5. Who had to get up from their seat and move to the back when whites got on the bus. But now I can sit at the front or anywhere else I choose to sit without having to move when someone Caucasian gets on the bus.

6. Who couldn't be out after dark in certain towns, or they would be lynched or shot because they were referred to as a "coon." But now I can go to any state, city, or town after dark without having to worry about a curfew or being killed.

7. Who had no choice but to live in a plantation shack owned by white people. But now I live in an upscale neighborhood with a lake in my backyard.

This is just a small portion of what your parents and foreparents went through also. This is why it is so important that we as a race become so much more considerate, thankful, grateful, and appreciative and not take for granted the struggles that our parents and foreparents went through. As a

race, and men who happen to be black, we must also make the right choices and take advantage of every opportunity that our parents and foreparents made possible for our generation.

As I bring this book to a close, I am truly and sincerely grateful, thankful, and appreciative to God, who is first and foremost head of my life, and to my parents and foreparents. Because of them, I am a God-fearing, professional, educated, successful man with morals and values, who happens to be black.

Now that you have read this book,

You are no longer in bondage.

Your shackles have been taken off,

So you are now free to go,

A new person,

With a new mentality, thought process, and
mindset,

With a new destiny,

With a newfound success.

Take care and my prayer is that God will continue to pour his blessings upon you, that you
will not have room enough to receive them all.

ACKNOWLEDGMENTS

I WOULD LIKE TO FIRST ACKNOWLEDGE my Lord and Savior Jesus Christ, who is head of my life and made all of this possible by putting every word in my heart and spirit to write. I would like to thank my mother, Ruby Bolden, who is my hero and my heart. A special thanks to my brother, Marcus Bolden, who is my number-one fan and always encourages me. Also a special thanks to Denise Baker and Erika Paradis for their time, effort, and support. I would like to thank my son, Brian Raleigh, who is also my biggest fan. I would like to thank other family members and friends: Warren Bolden, Louis Bolden, Cheryl Bolden, Arthur and Satonia Prevost, Daryl Harrison, Jessica Pokluda, Carolyn Cross, Patricia Price, Felicia Drake, Margaret Rhoades, James Mitchell, Kenneth Johnson, James Pope, Cedric Dave, Derrick Fontel Leon, James Green, Allan Wright, Lyndon James, George W. Sanders, Dwayne Kidd, Julie Tuttle, Curtis Knight, Willie Washington, Elmer Fisher, Eric Jeffries, Stan Connally, and the hundreds of wonderful people who took the time out of their busy schedules to talk to me for this book. Lastly, I thank and appreciate all of the other parents and foreparents for their struggles which ultimately gave me the opportunity to become a man, who happens to be black.

COMMENTS AND THOUGHTS WELCOMED!

I hope you have enjoyed reading my book as much as I have enjoyed writing it. I also hope that it has helped you to become a better person in every aspect of your life, because we all have room for improvement. Please feel free to share your comments or thoughts by mail or e-mail. Take care, may God continue to bless you, and I look forward to hearing from you soon.

BRIAN BOLDEN
P.O. BOX 691951
HOUSTON, TX 77269-1951

E-MAIL ADDRESS:
happens2bblack@yahoo.com

www.ingramcontent.com/pod-product-compliance
Lightning Source LLC
Chambersburg PA
CBHW020257290526
45784CB00003B/1275